8
REALLY
RELEVANT
SUPER
SIGNIFICANT
PROMISES
FOR TEENAGERS
WHO WANT TO
FALL IN LOVE
WITH JESUS
FOREVER .

Dan & Dave
Davidson

New Leaf Press

First Printing: May 1999

Copyright © 1998 Dan & Dave Davidson ThinkWOW.com.

ISBN: 0-89221-460-0
Library of Congress Catalog#: 99-64016

Printed in the United States of America

Cover Design by: Left Coast Designs,Portland, OR

Interior Design by: Janell Robertson

Unless otherwise noted, Bible Scripture is from the New International Version Copyright 1973, 1978, 1984 International Bible Society.

The "Wow, Click, Zap" bible study method, Verse Rehearse™, Eternal Journal™, the "Think WOW" plan, The 8 Promises™, the phrase "Fall In Love With Jesus Forever™, P.O.W.E.R. Prayer Inspire Me Biography™, are trademarks of Dan and Dave Davidson, ThinkWow.com.

Dedicated
to those we have partnered
with in Youth Ministry

Check out more cool stuff
on the 8 P.R.O.M.I.S.E.S. at
8Promises.com

PRAYER RELATIONSHIPS OBEDIENCE MINISTRY IMAGE SEX ETERNITY SCRIPTURE

Prayer

I WILL ALWAYS PRAY.
Cultivate devotion with God

Relationships

I WILL LOVE GOD & OTHERS.
Celebrate family & friends

Obedience

I WILL FOLLOW JESUS.
Initiate God's will

Ministry

I WILL SHARE MY FAITH.
Duplicate & disciple

Image

I WILL BE CONFIDENT IN CHRIST.
Imitate Christ's identity

Sex

I WILL SAVE SEX FOR MARRIAGE.
Demonstrate purity

Eternity

I WILL MEASURE MY LIFE.
Evaluate your life story

Scripture

I WILL GROW IN GOD'S WORD.
Activate faith

Cheeseburger Prayers

A steaming made-to-order cheeseburger with extra mayonnaise was competing with an equally greasy order of fries. As I prayed a "fast food grace" it dawned on me that soon I would enter high school hallways as a freshman.

Dear Lord, thanks for the food You've blessed me with today. And God . . . since I start high school next week, I figure that the next four years will affect the rest of my life. So, please guide me in a special way. Reveal to me whatever it is that is important to You. Thanks for listening. Amen.

That was it. The prayer that changed my life. That cheeseburger plea was a spiritual milestone. God answered that prayer in ways I never thought possible.

Just weeks later I began attending a dynamic youth group. Every week I learned more about the Lord and His unwavering love for me.

I can thank God for over a half dozen very important spiritual mentors in my life, including my brother Dan who took me to his youth group meetings when I was in junior high. God can use others to help mold us into His image.

It may take more than a fast food prayer, but I urge you to open your heart to God and ask Him to direct His plans for your life. Ask Him to provide a mentor to walk with you as you walk with God. He will faithfully lead you and guide you.

I remembered the first lesson I had shared with youth at my church about what King Solomon had learned after having it all. *"Remember your Creator in the days of your youth, before the days of trouble come . . . Now all has been heard; here is the conclusion of the matter: Fear God and keep his commandments, for this is the whole duty of man."* Ecclesiastes 12:1,13

The secret to falling in love with Jesus forever is to honor Him fearfully, keeping His promises faithfully.

— DAVE DAVIDSO

We are shaped and fashioned by what we love.

GOETHE

Falling In Love With Jesus Forever

One of the underlying themes of the Bible is a metaphor that presents Christ as a groom and His church as a bride. In heaven, Christ and His church will come together in a wedding banquet and feast to celebrate a reunion of love and commitment for eternity.

Proposal: Christ has already given His "wedding" proposal to each and every one of us. He came to earth, died for our sins and was resurrected and is now in heaven. His invitation is simple . . . "Will you be united with Me in perfect love forever?"

God invites each one of us to become a part of His kingdom. He has already revealed His wedding vows in His Word as part of godly promises and covenants.

Engagement: Perhaps you are only engaged to Christ with a tentative commitment for the future. "Yeah, maybe in a couple of years we'll get together, Jesus." The Holy Spirit continues to give you the invitation from Christ to become one with Him, but we often keep pushing back the wedding date because we're not ready to fully commit. Move up the wedding date to today!

Wedding: It's time to say I DO, I WILL to Jesus. Just as God has given us His promises, there are foundational promises and vows that we can commit to today to become one with the Lord. First, we need to accept His proposal and say, "I DO."

Once you commit to Christ, it's time for the wedding vows to be lived out the rest of your life here on earth. The secret to falling in love with Jesus forever is to honor Him fearfully, keeping His promises faithfully.

Don't be late for your own wedding day! If you don't make it to the church on time, you won't be able to attend the wedding banquet and feast Jesus is planning for you in heaven.   — DAN DAVIDSON

It makes me cry when
I realize how much Jesus loves me.
And still to this day, it amazes me that
He loves us so much He would die for us!
REBECCA ST. JAMES

What Does It Take To Fall In Love?

Our biggest dreams in life usually include wanting to fall in love. We look for love that is true and long lasting. What does it take to fall in love with someone? How can it become a "forever love?"

Some of the same relationship components that are present in dating, in friendship, and even in families can give us insight into how we can fall in love with Jesus forever.

If you really seek Jesus and pursue Him with your whole heart, His love will never fail you. He will never let you down. A love relationship with Jesus only grows stronger because it is always backed by His perfect character.

It's our commitment and initiative that fall short. He is always there to forgive, to comfort and to love us unconditionally. Faithful promises that we make and keep are pillars of commitment that help sustain a lifelong devotion for Jesus. It's a love that will always keep growing as long as we keep walking in His ways.

— DAVE DAVIDSON

8 P.R.O.M.I.S.E.S.
**Prayer • Relationships • Obedience • Ministry
Image • Sex • Eternity • Scripture**

Our **prayer** life is nurtured as much as it is watered with experience. Our **relationships** are blessed according to the devotional investment we give to God. We can live in **obedience** to God as we realize He is the Master and we are His servants.

We share our faith in **ministry** as we understand God's unconditional love for all people in His kingdom. Our personal victories are linked to our **image** in Christ and the truths we live daily. Our purity regarding **sex** is based on our devotion to keeping God's commandments.

A reality check for **eternity** comes as we realize that we are not of this world, but are citizens of heaven. Our study and meditation of **scripture** reveals our hunger and thirst for God's Word to become our life story.

As we truly desire a relationship with Jesus, we begin to fall in love with Him. The more we come to know the nature of Jesus, the more devoted we will become. To know Jesus intimately is to fall in love with Him forever.

We know God only as far as we love Him.
BERNARD OF CLAIRAUX

**Did the fact ever cross your
mind that you are here in this
world just to understand the
LORD JESUS CHRIST,
and for no other reason?**
GEORGE MACDONALD

We obey God because He is the sovereign Lord of the universe and our obedience is the only acceptable response to His unspeakable kindness.
DR. KEITH PHILLIPS

Ready, Set, Grow!

God and His angels in heaven are very excited that you picked this book up and have started reading. Any resource that reflects God's Word and gives Him glory can be a powerful tool in the supernatural.

One of the last things the devil wants you to do is read a book about falling in love with Jesus. He will most likely try to discourage and distract you, but God is ready to arm you for battle. Now is the time to measure Gods' promises and see how they can impact your life forever.

You are a few chapters away from being able to set meaningful goals and godly objectives in your life. God loves you and is ready to bless you. Welcome to a spiritual training program especially for you! **Here's a simple challenge** - Finish reading this book!

One barrier that you may need to conquer is time. If you can't find the time, trim your T.V. viewing by 10% this next week. Consider tithing a sitcom or a rerun to learn more about how God's Word and His promises can change your life.

Thirty minutes a day adds up to one week a year of waking time. Suddenly, things like standing in line, extra time in the bathroom and watching TV can seem insignificant. The thought that we may spend a week of each year doing such trivial things should catch our attention.

If you average eight hours of sleep a night, by age 75 you will have spent 25 years in bed. So, with that 50 waking years that we have, minus our childhood, we need to redeem the time (Ephesians 5:17) we have left in life.

You will be richly blessed when you set time aside for daily study and devotion to God. But don't stop there . . . why not fellowship in God's Word all day long. In Psalm 119 the psalmist says that *"he praises the Lord seven times a day for His righteous laws."*

There are verses throughout the book of Psalms that speak of the blessings of daily time spent with God. Psalm 34:8 says, *"Blessed is the man who listens to Me, who watches daily at My doors."* James 4:8 says, *"Draw near to Me and I will draw near to you."*

Instead of surfing channels on the tube, you can choose to serve God and glorify Him with . . . love, joy, peace, patience, kindness, goodness, faithfulness, gentleness and self-control (Galatians 5:22-23). Don't devote your soul to the remote control, but to God's control.

— DAVE DAVIDSON

P— R— O— M— I— S— E— S—

Keep this promise . . .

Prayer

I WILL ALWAYS PRAY
Cultivate devotion
with God.

Pray continually
(1 Thessalonians 5:17).

Prayer is talking to God. It's that simple. God fully understands the desires of our heart even before we begin to pray. You have the opportunity every day to instantly communicate with the Creator of the universe.

Why don't we pray more often? Surveys indicate that even pastors average only a few minutes of prayer each day. Surely the devil realizes the awesome power of prayer and does everything he can to divert our attention to the things of the world.

God is always pleased when we're on our knees. He loves to fellowship with His people. God wants a loving relationship with you. He wants to hear all your thoughts, dreams and fears.

Prayer is always heart changing and the heart that God wants to change is yours. Take time to talk with God as you walk with Him. — DAVE DAVIDSON

PRAYER IS
A CONSTANT JOURNEY
OF DISCOVERY & LEARNING.
FEEL FREE TO QUESTION,
TO EXPERIMENT, &
ALWAYS BE YOURSELF.
HE WILL MEET YOU
WHERE YOU ARE AT
REGARDLESS OF
YOUR PRACTICE.
DAVE DAVIDSON

In Your Face GRACE

The disciples in the garden of Gesthemane couldn't stay awake three times to support Jesus when He was praying, but **God's Grace** later enabled them to be witnesses as pillars on which the early church was built.

Think of a missed quiet time with God like standing Him up for a date.
MARY GREER

Therefore, since we are receiving a kingdom
that cannot be shaken, let us be thankful, and so
worship God acceptably with reverence and awe.

HEBREWS 12:28

Seven times a day I praise you . . .

PSALM 119:164

Prayer Is A Habit . . . Don't Break It, Grab It!

Psalm 119:64 describes an attitude of prayer that is continuous . . . seven times a day. When was the last time you praised God seven times in one day?

Experts say that it takes at least 21 days to form a new habit or break an old one. Make prayer a daily habit today.

Think of everyday activities as prayer triggers. At a stop light you could pray to stop sin and selfishness in your life. When you brush your teeth pray for a clean, pure heart.

Whenever you see a telephone, remember that God's direct line to heaven is always open. When the phone rings, say a prayer for the caller. Pray for all the people mentioned in newspaper stories you read. Always listen to God. He will prompt you to pray when your heart is open to Him.

Try some of these prayer triggers for the next 21 days. Making prayer a daily habit could be the most significant life-changing thing you do as a teen.

— DAVE DAVIDSON

CAN YOU SAY THIS TO GOD?

I have been driven many times to my knees by the overwhelming conviction that I had nowhere else to go; my own wisdom, that of all around me, seem insufficient for the day.

ABRAHAM LINCOLN

**Prayer is like
a bungee cord
attached to heaven.
Each time you jump out
and experience new
adventures in life,
you stay connected
and always bounce
back to God.**
DAN DAVIDSON

People often ask, "Why do you insist on prayer so much?" The answer is very simple — because Jesus did. Jesus, the annointed of God, made prayer His custom. Paul, with his background and intellect, depended on prayer because he said he was weak. David, the king, called himself a poor man and cried to the Lord. Hannah prayed for a son and gave birth to a prophet.

LEONARD RAVENHILL

God imaginatively created us with the capacity to fellowship with Him despite our obvious differences in holiness. This potential interaction with a living God should never be taken for granted.

He has made everything beautiful in its time. He has also set eternity in the hearts of men; yet they cannot fathom what God has done from beginning to end. (Ecclesiastes 3:11)

Over the years life can put a squeeze on our spiritual passions. Many would-be devoted followers of Christ fail to draw on the Holy Spirit's power. Even though we are created for fellowship with a living God, we often become passive with the privilege.

When His presence goes unnoticed, we live without the best thing going for us . . . Jesus. This miscue is a misadventure filled with calamity and chaos. We need to discover daily the blessings of a great God.

How could any relationship be maintained if no time was spent together? Without a shared personal time there is no intimate understanding, no growing faith, no maturing love. How can you know God's plans for your life without feeding on His word regularly?

True fulfillment in life is not experienced unless we do what our creator intended. Ask God today to help you be thankful for His precious communion. Begin to develop a dynamic daily discipline of prayer and devotion that honors Him.

A growing love relationship with God will give your spiritual life an energized edge that will last for eternity.   — DAVE DAVIDSON

INSPIRE ME BIOGRAPHY™

GEORGE MUELLER, a bible distributor, preacher and missionary to orphans in the 1800's, logged 50,000 specific answers to prayer in his journal. Five thousand of these were answered on the very day of their asking.

Proclaim His Names

ALPHA, ALMIGHTY, AUTHORITY ,
CHRIST the SAVIOUR, WISDOM WELLSPRING
CREATOR, COUNSELOR, CARPENTER —
COMPASSIONATE COMFORTER,

MAKER, MESSIAH, MAJESTY,
MOST HIGH MASTER, the KING of KINGS
REDEEMER, REFINER, RENEWER, TRUTH TEACHER,
TRIUMPHANT, WORSHIPPED, BREAD of LIFE, PERFECTER
SON of MAN, the BRIGHT and MORNING STAR,

RULER, RESCUER, RESTORER, SERVANT SAVIOUR,
SOUL DEFENDER, REPROOFER, REFORMER
AWESOME GOD / REVELATION
KINSMAN, INEFFABLE, ALL COMFORT, APPOINTED HEIR,
THE COMING ONE, PARDONER SPIRIT, SILENT SHIELD,
SALVATION, GRACIOUS GIVER, WATER of LIFE
SOVEREIGN, SUFFICIENT, HOPE,
POWER, RECEIVER, EXAMINER, BARRIER BREAKER,
INFINITE, INDWELLING, EXAMPLE,

FOUNDATION, FORERUNNER, FRIEND of SINNERS,
CHOSEN, MINISTER, GOVERNOR, CONSOLATION,
CONQUEROR, CRUCIFIED, LEADER, LAWGIVER,
QUICKENER, INHERITANCE, INTERCESSOR
INCARNATE, ISRAEL'S JOY, TENDER — GOOD GOD,
GUARDIAN, ENCOURAGER, EXCELLENT COMPANION,
VISION, UPLIFTER, SUPREME STRENGTH,
REFUGE, RANSOM, OUR VICTORY,
ETERNAL, GOOD SHEPHERD,

PRAISEWORTHY, JUST JUDGE, KIND KING
PREACHER, CROWN JEWEL, EAGLE'S WING,
BOUNDLESS, BOUNTIFUL, BEAUTIFUL — MAGNIFICENT
DESTINATION, ALWAYS THERE, ELOHIM, DEBT PAYER, POTTER.
NEEDED, FELLOW FRIEND, HUSBANDMAN, UNCREATED,
UNDEFEATED,PEARL OMNISCIENT, VANQUISHER,
ALL REIGNING, REFRESHER, REDEMPTION, ROCK,
RESURRECTION, REJOICING, REPAIRER, ROOT,

I AM ,
LEAST of THESE, HOPE of GLORY, PRECIOUS PROPHET,
JEHOVAH, PROVIDER, PRINCE of PEACE,
GOOD GUIDE, GREAT GIFT, ONLY BEGOTTEN, BELOVED SON
ALTOGETHER LOVELY CHRIST, STRONG STANDARD,
SWEETER SPIRIT, NEW SONG, SANCTUARY, TABERNACLE,
BUILDER, FRUITBEARER, DESTROYER,
QUELLER of STORMS, HEAD OF THE CHURCH,
OLIVE TREE, NAZARENE

YAHWEH

GOD of CHERUBIM, HOPE of HOPES,
STAR of JACOB, PASSOVER LAMB, SUPPLIER,
SUCCORER, SHEKINAH, HUMAN, DIVINE,

PERFECT MAN

DAY SPRING, HOST CAPTAIN, ROOT of DAVID, ROSE of SHARON
PRINCE of LIFE, WORD of GOD, ATONEMENT,
MANNA, POWER, SHIELD, YEARNED FOR, ADVOCATE,
PERFECT WILL, HALLOWED be Thy NAME,
APPROVED, APOSTLE, ADONAI, ARM of the LORD,
ANCIENT of DAYS, ANOINTED, ABOUNDING, FIRST BORN BABE,
SHILOH, TRANSFIGURED, ALL POWERFUL MESSENGER,

KING of the JEWS

OINTMENT, VERITY, YOKE FELLOW, OMNIPOTENT,
OMNIPRESENT, WORTHY, WARRIOR, BURDEN BEARER,
JESSE'S ROOT, LIVING ONE, YESTERDAY, TODAY,
TOMORROW, MANSION MAKER, OMEGA, OVERCOMER,
INVINCIBLE, INFALLIBLE — WORD, WINE, WAY,
IMMORTAL, THIEF OF NIGHT, EVERLASTING

EMMANUEL, ENDURING, EXALTED, EL SHADDIA

LORD, LIGHT, LOVE, LIFE,

TREASURE, MEASURELESS, SANCTIFICATION, PIERCED,
SALT, SABBATH, HELMET, BELT of TRUTH,
UNCHANGEABLE, UNMOVEABLE, RANSOM,
LORD of LORDS, DISCIPLER, LIGHT of the WORLD,

OBEDIENT, FATHER'S SON, PHYSICIAN,
ANGEL OF THE LORD, ALL IN ALL, SUFFERER,
SPRING OF JOY, DESIRE, SOON BRIDEGROOM

RIGHTEOUSNESS,

HOLY ONE, HIDING PLACE, FOUNTAIN, FATHER,
RIGHT HAND, PRECIOUS LAMB, OFFERING, MERCIFUL,
GLORIFIED, AMAZING GRACE, SOLID ROCK,
RISEN LORD, FISHER of MEN,

JESUS,

DWELLING PLACE, CORNERSTONE,
NAME ABOVE NAMES, WONDERFUL

Friendship With God

Have you ever loved someone so much that it hurt?
It physically ached because they cared for you in a
"different" way? "I love you, but I'm not **in** love with you"?
Do you remember how that felt? Magnify
that, and that's how God feels when we don't love
Him like he wants us to. All He asks for is our love,
while always giving His best to us.

ANGIE CUNDIFF

We are not told that Jesus ever taught His
disciples how to preach, but He taught them how
to pray. He wanted them to have power with God,
then He knew they would have power with men.

D.L. MOODY

INSPIRE ME BIOGRAPHY™

DAVID BRAINERD was a young American who had a severe case of tuberculosis; his weight dropped to 95 pounds. In his diary he wrote, "I got up this morning and the Indians were still committing adultery and drinking and beating their tom-toms and shouting like hell itself. I prayed from a half-hour after sunrise to a half-hour before sunset. There was nowhere to pray in the Indian camp. I went into the woods and knelt in the snow. It was up to my chin. I wrestled in prayer until a half-hour before sunset, and I could only touch the snow with the tips of my fingers. The heat of my body had melted the snow."

S.L.A.P.
SURVEY LIFE APPLY PRINCIPLE

Prayer does not equip us for greater works —
Prayer IS the greater work.

Oswald Chambers

W.O.R.S.H.I.P.

WORSHIP GOD IN SPIRIT AND IN TRUTH.
(John 4:24)

OBEY AND SERVE GOD.
(Matthew 4:10, Mark 10:45)

REJOICE IN THE LORD ALWAYS.
(Philippians 3:1)

SING PSALMS AND HYMNS.
(James 5:13 Colossians 3:16)

HAVE REVERENT FEAR.
(Hebrews 12:28,29; Revelations 14:7)

INTERCEDE AND PRAY TO GOD.
(1 Kings 13:6)

PRAISE GOD WITH SACRIFICE.
(Hebrews 13:15)

(P)— (R)— (O)— (M)— (I)— (S)— (E)— (S)—

Prayer
The Secret Of Falling In Love With Jesus Forever . . .
Honor Him Fearfully & Keep His Promises Faithfully

Keeping the promise **"I Will Always Pray"** gives God honor and glory He deserves, and also a reverence He demands. To have fear in the Lord means to be struck with supreme esteem . . . to admire and adore Him with awe and wonder.

A holy fear can be an incentive to repentance and can draw us closer to God. It is a reverent fear that links love and hope together. When you pray, remember that the King of kings who hears your requests and petitions is your faithful friend.

E-MAIL (ETERNAL-MAIL) FROM JESUS

To: teens@8promises.com

Thanks for praying today! I love to hear from you and your friends. You have an open line to heaven any time, anywhere. I am always by your side ready to listen, to comfort and to encourage you.

You are just beginning to experience the power of prayer. By keeping in touch every day, I will be able to show you the special plans I've prepared for your life.

Through prayer, you will also learn more about my perfect and complete love for you. Isn't falling in love awesome? Thanks for keeping the promise to always pray!

Your Faithful Friend, Jesus

Think WOW Promise Plan™

Think WOW: What if Jesus was your best friend in life? What if you talked to Him many times a day about your life through prayer and experienced His companionship, provision and friendship?

Make a VOW: Be committed to pray every day to Jesus. Despite distractions and diversions from the world, make a vow to always be devoted in daily prayer with God.

Plan HOW: Set aside a daily quiet time for prayer just as Jesus did. Take time for ten-second prayers. Create a plan for prayer; Develop pray triggers; Schedule it into your day.

Do it NOW: Say a prayer right now; talk to God now. Pray more than you ever have in your life in the next 24 hours. Don't put off or delay this powerful love link to God.

Push the PLOW: Keep on praying, day and night. Persistence with prayer will pay off in a love relationship with Jesus that will be more awesome than can be imagined.

Relationships

I WILL LOVE GOD & OTHERS
Celebrate family & friends

*Love the Lord your God with all your heart and with all
your soul and with all your mind and with all your
strength. . . . Love your neighbor as yourself.
There is no commandment greater than these*
(Mark 12:30,31).

The **three most important relationships** you
have are with God, your parents and your friends. Your life
now as a teen and in the future will center on these relationships with others.

Your Relationship With God: In the previous
chapter, prayer was discussed as a foundation to a deep
loving relationship with God. The Bible encourages us to
"love the Lord God with all our heart, soul and mind."
Spend time with Jesus everyday. Get to know Him and
love Him.

Your Relationship With Parents: Listen up! Red
Alert! God thought this was so important, He made it one
of the 10 commandments. "Honor your father and mother."
God didn't say to "rebel against," "put down," "be sarcas-
tic with," "never listen to," or "tolerate" your parents.
God said to honor and obey them.

Your Relationship With Friends: Friends can be
a great source of growth and fellowship in your Christian
walk. As a teen, friends will naturally be a strong influence in your life. Be aware of the magnetic force of peer
pressure. Keep your relationships with friends in perspective. Remember that Jesus is the best friend you'll ever
have.   — DAN DAVIDSON

In Your Face
G R A C E

Saul didn't exactly love God and others
when he persecuted and killed God's people just because they were followers of
Christ, but **God's Grace** transformed him
into the Apostle Paul who became the
primary missionary of the early church.

P—
R—
O—

➤ S . L . A . P . ◄
SURVEY LIFE APPLY PRINCIPLE

M—

We are what we fill our minds with. If we're
serious about becoming like Jesus, we must
spend time with Him. . . . We need
to make decisions now to get serious about
God. We must use our lives for Him before
it's too late.

O—

I—

S—

E—

Rebecca St. James

S—

Do not be misled; bad company corrupts a good character.

I CORINTHIANS 15:33

How Parents See Things . . .

Children, obey your parents
in the Lord, for this is right.
"Honor your father and mother"-
which is the first commandment
with a promise —

EPHESIANS 6:1,2

At times you may think you know everything there is to know in life . . . but you really don't. You may also think your parents don't know anything about life . . . but they know a lot.

You really start to show your smarts when you can admit you still have a lot to learn. Believe it or not, your parents have a lot they can teach you — if you're willing to learn from them.

They love you, and want to lead you, guide you, help you and teach you how to make it on your own. It takes a big person, as a teenager, to let them teach and lead.

Remember, Jesus was a teenager once. He was an exceptional one, but He was still a teenager. God knows what it's like to be in your place. He included an important principle as one of His ten commandments, "Honor your father and your mother."

Jesus honored and respected His father and mother as a teenager. With an open, loving heart, God can empower you to do the same today. — DAVE DAVIDSON

TEENAGERS,
are you tired of being harassed by your STUPID parents? Act now! Move out. Get a job and pay your own bills. Do it now while you still know everything.

When I was a boy of 14, my father was so ignorant I could hardly stand to have the old man around. But when I got to be 21, I was astonished at how much he had learned in seven years.

MARK TWAIN

Submit to one another
out of reverence for Christ.

EPHESIANS 5:21

S . L . A . P .
SURVEY LIFE APPLY PRINCIPLE

Bear with each other and forgive whatever grievances you may have against one another. Forgive as the Lord forgave you.

COLOSSIANS 3:13

Why Hang Out Together?

The only way to have a friend is to be one.
RALPH WALDO EMERSON

The Christian walk was never intended to be a solo effort.

Even the Lone Ranger had a partner. Times of growth are often linked with trials, victories and moments that connect us with other people. We are urged to not stop meeting together. (Hebrews 10:24)

Because God's main priority is His children, He is delighted when we join together in fellowship. He is pleased when brothers dwell together in perfect unity. (Psalm 133:1) The connection of personal growth between you and others creates a foundation for a love relationship with Jesus.

There are many blessings in being part of a dynamic youth group. As a teen, a group of Christian friends can be a strong foundation of understanding and support.

Fellowship can be a supernatural spark in your Christian walk as a young person. Within small youth groups and peer groups, friendships will emerge that will last for years to come. Invest in the lives of others. Cultivate friendships with other Christian teens.

The bonds of love and companionship that are formed now can be a source of hope and blessing for a lifetime. The secret of successful friendships and involvement in a Christ-centered youth group community is to show up and let God do His thing.   — Dave Davidson

. . . our generation is constantly concerned with **what others think,** rather than **what God says** — and we are falling morally because of it. But if we learn to **trust God,** then we're worried only about what **He** thinks of us - and that's **the only way to live!**

REBECCA ST. JAMES

Ⓟ—
Ⓡ—
Ⓞ—
Ⓜ—
Ⓘ—
Ⓢ—
Ⓔ—
Ⓢ—

Why Hang Out Together and Develop Community in a
Cool Youth Group

It's a way God multiplies ministry!

We can be a blessing to others - Ephesians 5:17

It is part of God's plan for your life - Philippians 1:6

You can receive a sense of belonging - Proverbs 17:7

It can give others a sense of belonging - Romans 12:13

Good company encourages good morals - 1 Corinthians 15:33

It gives others a chance to be a blessing to you - 2 Peter 1:5-8

You will consistently receive encouragement - Philippians 2:1-5

It can be a place where you can be accepted - 1 Corinthians 3:4

Gatherings can be a forum for developing friendships - 1 Peter 1:8,9

It's a good alternative to staying home with your parents - Ephesians 6:1,2

People you know can learn about the saving love of Jesus - Titus 2:11

It's a good way to cruise chicks and scope out guys - Proverbs 18:22

You can share with and invest your life in others - 2 Thessalonians 2:8

A way to grow in your relationship with God - Colossians 3:1,2

Time together offers a refuge from the world - Romans 12:2

It's a great opportunity to glorify God while enabling the

Holy Spirit to produce fruit in our lives. - Galatians 5:22,23

Training in spiritual warfare - Ephesians 6:18-20

This Is What A Friend Is

The happiest miser on earth is the man who saves up every friend he can make.

Robert E. Sherwood

Friendship is one of the sweetest joys of life. Many might have failed beneath the bitterness of their trial had they not found a friend.

Charles Spurgeon

A friend is a present you give yourself.

Robert Louis Stevenson

Be kind and compassionate to one another, forgiving each other, just as in Christ God forgave you.

Ephesians 4:32

Figure out exactly what is hurting.
— Psalm 139:38,39

Observe and understand in light of the cross.
— Luke 23:34

Resolve to forgive by Christ's power within you.
— Matthew 9:6

Give God permission to control all emotional change.
— Matthew 6:12-15

Identify new positive ways to look at situations.
—Romans 8:28

Verify in your own heart that God will take care of it.
— Ezekiel 16:62,63

Erase what is owed to you as you release responsibility.
— Matthew 18:27

Never return to old perspective despite feelings.
— John 2:12

Eliminate grudges and forgive as you pray.
— Mark 11:25

Specifically communicate any appropriate message.
— James 5:20

Saturate yourself in the truth of God's mercy.
— Titus 3:4,5

If you, O LORD, kept a record
of sins, O Lord, who could stand?
But with you there is forgiveness;
therefore you are feared. I wait for
the LORD, my soul waits, and in
his word I put my hope.
Psalms 130:3-5

His mercy
extends
to those who fear him,
from generation to generation.
LUKE 1:50

**Now all has been heard;
here is the conclusion
of the matter:
Fear God and keep His
commandments,
for this is
the whole duty of man.**

ECCLESIASTES 12:13

P —
R —
O —
M —
I —
S —
E —
S —

Relationships
The Secret Of Falling In Love With Jesus Forever . . .
Honor Him Fearfully & Keep His Promises Faithfully

Relationship is what being a Christian is all about. When we realize that the Creator of the Universe wants to be our best Friend, a holy fear and reverence fills our heart.

Develop a legacy perspective for your friendships. Prayerfully commit your friends to God and ask Him to use you in their lives for encouragement. Create a lifelong friend prayer-list.

Ask God to give you a greater respect and love for your parents. Seek to understand where they are coming from in situations that challenge your growing independence.

E-MAIL (ETERNAL-MAIL) FROM JESUS

To: teens@8promises.com

It has been great to be loved by you this week. The love relationship between us is growing every day. Isn't it wonderful to love and to be loved? I've also noticed the love you've shown recently to your family and friends. You have set aside your own wishes for the interest of others.

That's sacrificial love! It's the kind of love I demon strated when I died on the cross for your sins . . . an unconditional love. Remember that my love for you is the same yesterday, today, and forever!

Your Bridegroom, Jesus

Think WOW Promise Plan™

Think WOW: What if you really loved God with your whole heart, mind, and soul? Think about the strong relationships that you'd have in your life if you loved others in the same way.

Make a VOW: Commit yourself today to serve God wholeheartedly and to "love your neighbor as yourself." Make this a lifelong promise and be devoted to keeping it forever.

Plan HOW: Make a list of the important relationships in your life. How can you strengthen ties with family, friends, neighbors, and classmates? Take steps to build deeper relationships.

Do it NOW: Don't waste one more minute of your life not loving God completely. Call someone today and tell them you love them. Act now; don't delay in loving God and others.

Push the PLOW: Recommit your life to God each day, drawing closer to Him. Rekindle relationships. With God's power persevere. When in doubt, keep on loving others with a devoted heart.

Keep this promise . . .

Obedience
I WILL FOLLOW JESUS
Initiate God's Will

*. . . being confident of this,
that he who began a good work in you
will carry it on to completion
until the day of Christ Jesus
(Philippians 1:6).*

You have already learned about the promises relating to prayer and relationships. Now it's decision time. Who will your heart be obedient to? Who are you going to follow in life?

The Bible tells us we can only serve or follow one person or thing at a time. We cannot serve God and the world. We have to choose one or the other.

If you want to fall in love with Jesus forever, the answer is simple . . . follow Him.

Jesus has a plan for your life. He has prepared the most awesome journey you could ever imagine. He has plans for you to prosper. Jesus knows where along the path He will need to protect you from harm, and when He will need to carry you.

Obey Jesus and follow His commandments. He is ready to love you, to guide you and to bless you abundantly. — DAN DAVIDSON

Finally be STRONG in the LORD and in his MIGHTY POWER.
Ephesians 6:10

There is no end to how far we can go in our relationship with Him, yet there are those who trust Christ for their salvation and go no further. The point of salvation is just the beginning of an incredible journey. . . . Often we reach a place of contentment and want to "pitch our tent" and remain there. But God desires for us to be mobile and ready to follow Him anywhere at any time. His timing is perfect, so, unless we are plugged in, we may miss the next exciting turn in this race.

BOB HARTMAN

P— R— O— M— I— S— E— S—

ARE YOU
BROKEN BEFORE GOD?

ARE YOU willing to surrender your rights to God and allow Him to be in control of your life? **ARE YOU** rejecting old thought patterns and feelings that contradict your new life in Christ? **ARE YOU** obedient to God with motives of love? **ARE YOU** actively letting Christ produce fruit in your life by being faithful to Him?

ARE YOU willing to live simply, to lessen your will, to be exposed and to be rejected by the world? **ARE YOU** ready to draw upon Christ's strength rather than your own? **ARE YOU** seeking Christ Himself more than the benefits He gives in heaven? **ARE YOU** depending on God for your basic need of a fulfilling life of purpose?

ARE YOU quick and sincere to repent? **ARE YOU** identifying your self-image with His identity? **ARE YOU** forgiving yourself and others? **ARE YOU** transparent and vulnerable? **ARE YOU** willing to share wounds of weakness, stories of struggles and fears of failures to help others grow?

ARE YOU willing to let others get the credit? **ARE YOU** spending time in prayer? **ARE YOU** yielding your finances to God and trusting Him about money? **ARE YOU** giving your time, talent and resources for His glory? **ARE YOU** keeping the faith by sharing it with others?

ARE YOU teachable? **ARE YOU** humble before God? **ARE YOU** ready to serve God? **ARE YOU** willing to be misunderstood? **ARE YOU** willing to be broken again and again? **ARE YOU** willing to be made anew in Christ?

— DAVE DAVIDSON

THE HOLY SPIRIT

Jesus promised us that He would send a Counselor, the **HOLY SPIRIT**. The **HOLY SPIRIT** is the Spirit of faith, fire, and glory of God. The **HOLY SPIRIT** is the Spirit of Jesus Christ, the Spirit of judgement, justice and life.

The **HOLY SPIRIT** illuminates knowledge and the fear of the Lord. The **HOLY SPIRIT** is the Spirit of the Sovereign Lord as well as grace and supplication.

The **HOLY SPIRIT** is the Spirit of truth, of wisdom, and of understanding. The Spirit of the living God is the Spirit of wisdom, revelation, and sonship, which is adoption into God's kingdom.

The **HOLY SPIRIT** is the gift, the breath, and the voice of Almighty God. He is the Spirit of counsel, of power, and of holiness. The promised **HOLY SPIRIT** is a seal and deposit guaranteeing our inheritance.

— DAVE DAVIDSON

Without an adequate knowledge of God's Word, a disciple is gambling his future on feelings, hopes, and opinions, instead of securing it in God's will and the facts of His faith. . . . We are empowered to consistently obey God through our knowledge of Scripture and our surrendered will. . . . Most Christians want to obey God's Word, but wanting is not enough. Wanting is often a function of your emotions. It fluctuates with your feelings. The disciple wills to obey God's Word.

DR. KEITH PHILLIPS

SERVE, ACCEPT, FORGIVE, HONOR, TEACH, SUBMIT, GREET, AND **ENCOURAGE** ONE ANOTHER. BE DEVOTED WITH **ONE ANOTHER**. BEAR ONE ANOTHER'S BURDENS. **LOVE ONE ANOTHER**.

SYNOPSIS OF SEVERAL BIBLE VERSES

The Nerve To Serve

You will find, as you look back upon your life, that the moments that stand out are the moments when you have done things for others.

HENRY DRUMMOND

Endure hardship with us like a good soldier of Christ Jesus. Therefore I endure everything for the sake of the elect, that they too may obtain the salvation that is in Christ Jesus, with eternal glory.

2 TIMOTHY 2:3,4,10

P—
R—
O—
M—
I—
S—
E—
S—

In Your Face
G R A C E

Jonah outright defied God and disobeyed Him when God asked him to share his faith with the city of Nineveh, but **God's Grace** saved Jonah from the belly of a giant fish and enabled him to repent and preach to the city which resulted in revival.

Leaving Idols Idle

Our hearts seem to gravitate toward the things of the world. Even in the midst of miracles from God, we often look for other things to serve, worship and honor.

While Moses was on Mount Sinai receiving the Ten Commandments from God, the Israelites created an idol and worshipped the golden calf. They were impatient and their devotion quickly turned away from God to the world and their own desires.

What idols have you created in your life while you are waiting for God? Even good things can become idols. Are you honoring friends, music, school, sports or even your family more than God?

It's time to turn away from the idols in your life and remember the covenant of love God made for us through Jesus. — DAN DAVIDSON

He's the Master, we're the servants. He's the General, we're the soldiers. If you're really a Christian, you're at the beck and command of the King.

If Jesus decided to go the way of least pain, He would have never gone to the cross. There is no place of greater blessing for you than in the center of God's will. You must stop to count the cost, but remember one thing — the privilege of serving God always outweighs the price!

KEITH GREEN

If anyone wishes to come after Me, let him deny himself, and take up his cross, and follow Me. For whoever wishes to save his life shall lose it; but whoever loses his life for My sake and the Gospel's shall save it.

Mark 8:34-35

One half of knowing what you want is knowing
what you must give up before you get it.
SIDNEY HOWARD

Following in Faith

Once a large crowd witnessed a daring man walk across the chasm of Niagara Falls on a dangling tightrope. After successfully making it across and back again, the man asked, "Is there anyone here who doesn't believe that I can walk across the rope again?"

The crowd convinced of his heroics, all agreed saying, "We believe you can." Then the tightrope walker asked the crowd, "Then who will go across with me as I carry them?" Despite their "belief" no one was willing to cross over. No one had enough faith.

Are You Banking It All On Jesus? Jesus saved Peter in the water reaching out His hand saying, *"You of little faith, why did you doubt?"* (Matthew 14:31)

Are you willing to drop obstacles in your life that may come between you and God? Are invisible idols robbing God of His fullest glory in your life? Are your mountains movable?

How BIG is your God? The term "doubting Thomas" comes from John 20:24-29 where Thomas had been out buying munchies at 7-11. The other disciples claimed, "We have seen the Lord!" But Thomas said to them, "Unless I see the nail marks in His hands and put my finger where the nails were, and put my hand into His side, I will not believe it."

Jesus, appearing later, said to Thomas, *"Put your finger here; see my hands. Reach out your hand and put it into my side. Stop doubting and believe."* Thomas said to him, "My Lord and my God!" Then Jesus told him, *"Because you have seen me, you have believed; blessed are those who have not seen and yet have believed."*

We won't be able to put our hands into the actual wounds of Jesus or gain a glimpse of God on a mountain, but is evidence really a luxury? Wouldn't you rather take Jesus on His word and enjoy the benefits of living by faith? — DAVE DAVIDSON

We live by FAITH, not by sight.
2 Corinthians 5:7

FLEE THE EVIL DESIRES OF YOUTH, AND PURSUE RIGHTEOUSNESS, FAITH, LOVE AND PEACE, ALONG WITH THOSE WHO CALL ON THE LORD OUT OF A PURE HEART.
2 TIMOTHY 2:22

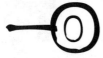

COST OF THE
CROSS

Do not conform any longer
to the pattern of this world, but be
transformed by the renewing of your mind.
Then you will be able to test and approve
what God's will is — his good, pleasing
and perfect will.

ROMANS 12:2

Commit your soul to God.
— 1 Peter 4:19; Jude 21
Obey God rather than man.
— Acts 5:29
Make straight paths for your feet.
—Hebrews 12:13
Make sure you're filled with the Spirit.
— Ephesians 5:18
Imitate Christ.
— Ephesians 5:1,2; James 4:7
Train yourself to be godly.
— 1 Timothy 4:7

Yield to Christ.
— Proverbs 3:5,6; Romans 12:1
Overcome sin.
— 1 Corinthians 10:13; 1 Pet. 5:8,9
Understand God's plan.
— Jeremiah 29:13; 33:3
Receive God's strength.
— 2 Peter 1:2-4; Philippians 4:13
Stand firm in the faith.
— 1 Corinthians 16:13
Everything for Jesus.
— Colossians 3:17
Live by faith.
— Hebrews 10:23,38; 11:6
Fear God.
— Hebrews 12:28,29; 1 Pet. 2:17

**If anyone
would come after me,
he must deny himself
and take up his cross
and follow me.**

MARK 8:34   LUKE 9:23

CAN YOU SAY
THIS TO GOD?

Teach me your way, O LORD, and I will walk in YOUR truth;
give me an undivided heart, that I may fear YOUR name.

PSALM 86:11

As a true believer you are God's child. Jesus is within you. To you, to everyone, He is saying, "I want to be your Lord, I want to be the king of your life. I want to control your time, your talents, your money, your holidays, your work, your marriage. Come to me, to the foot of the cross, and make me Lord of your life."

GEORGE VERWER

In Daniel 3:18, Shadrach, Meshach and Abednego told the king that even if God wouldn't deliver them from the furnace, they still would not bow to the king's statue of gold. Wow! What an uncompromising message! Even to the point of death, they were willing to pay the price for radically following God. God didn't deliver them from the furnace, but in the midst of it.

REBECCA ST. JAMES

Many are called, but few get 'up.

OLIVER HERFORD

"FOR I KNOW THE PLANS I HAVE FOR YOU," DECLARES THE LORD, "PLANS TO PROSPER AND NOT HARM YOU, PLANS TO GIVE YOU HOPE AND A FUTURE."

JEREMIAH 29:11

Make Sure of Your Calling!
Therefore, my brothers,
be all the more eager
to make your CALLING and election sure.
For if you do these things, YOU WILL NEVER
FALL, and you will receive a rich welcome
into the ETERNAL KINGDOM of our Lord
and Savior Jesus Christ.

2 PETER 2:10,11

Above all,
Love each other deeply,
because love covers over
a multitude of sins.
1 PETER 4:8

O Obedience
The Secret Of Falling In Love With Jesus Forever . . .
Honor Him Fearfully & Keep His Promises Faithfully

Godly obedience requires a deep desire and great personal initiative. God is literally waiting for you to take Him up on His promises.

Jesus is calling for young people who are willing to pay the price of deep fellowship with Him. We need to enlist in a spiritual training program to become godly. (1 Timothy 4:7)

Schoolwork, dating, music, sports, or anything else can stand in the way of you and God. Even good things that demand more attention can distract us and become a diversion. When you fall in love with Jesus your heart won't be as likely to drift away.

E-MAIL (ETERNAL-MAIL) FROM JESUS

To: teens@8promises.com

I know how challenging it can be to do the right thing in every situation . . . to obey your parents, to respect authority, to stay away from sin, and to live a holy life.

I lived on earth and experienced all the same feelings and temptations. I always followed my Father and He was always there for me just as I am always here for you today.

I've gone before you and prepared a path of holiness. Follow me and I will lead you. Obey my commandments and I will bless you. Every step is worth it. My love for you will never stop. Thanks for your heart of devotion!

Your Shepherd, Jesus

Think WOW Promise Plan™

Think WOW: What would your Christian walk be like if you obeyed God with the same level of faith that Noah did? Imagine experiencing God's blessings by always following Jesus.

Make a VOW: Just like a wedding vow, make a pledge to follow Jesus in sickness and in health, and for richer or poorer. Cling to God's perfect promise of love that He will never break.

Plan HOW: Make a list of the major areas of your life . . . home, school, church, family, friends. Write down steps to follow Jesus more completely. Identify areas where you need to be more obedient.

Do it NOW: Be obedient today. Review the 10 commandments and put them into practice. In every decision you make follow God's purpose for your life. Don't put off living a life of faith and obedience.

Push the PLOW: Always keep your eyes on God's prize. Don't look back. Keep your hands and heart to the plow of faith. Follow Jesus with a whole heart. Look ahead and keep pressing.

Keep this promise . . .

Ministry

I WILL SHARE MY FAITH
Duplicate & disciple

*Therefore go and make disciples of all nations,
baptizing them in the name of the Father and of
the Son and of the Holy Spirit, and teaching them
to obey everything I have commanded you. And surely
I am with you always, to the very end of the age*
(Matthew 28:19, 20).

You may not realize it yet, but the greatest task of your life is before you now — the greatest challenge of history is just around the corner.

Now is the time for a crash course on God's heart. He wants you to take personal ownership in the Great Commission.

God's Word sets forth an urgent missionary call that will melt church pews into starting blocks of service in the race of faith . . . if your heart is willing.

It's time to jump from the bleachers and dash into eternity. There's no time for sugar coating. Naptime is not promoted. There's only time for God's compassionate truth. As Leonard Ravenhill says, "The church has many organizers, but few agonizers."

Listen to God's call to witness to others and allow the Holy Spirit to confront and convict your heart. Seek first His kingdom and His righteousness, and all these things will be given to you as well (Matthew 6:33.)

Some may mistake the devil's line that you can't be involved in the missionary journey. But, God has a part for everyone in His mission plan.

He is so flexible, so innovative, so powerful, so patient, so purposeful that He will empower you with His Spirit when you are ready. You need to be willing to get your feet wet and walk with Him.

So dare to answer His call to action. Dare to make a world of difference. Dare to make your great ambition God's Great Commission. — DAN & DAVE DAVIDSON

**But you will receive power
when the Holy Spirit comes
on you; and you will be my
witnesses in Jerusalem,
and in all Judea and Samaria,
and to the ends of the earth.**

ACTS 1:8

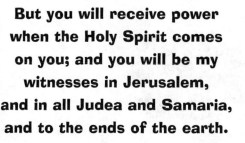

GOD'S GREAT AMBITION

For Christ's love
COMPELS US,
**because we are convinced that one
died for all, and therefore all died.**

2 CORINTHIANS 5:14

The difference between catching men

and catching fish is

that you catch fish that are alive,

and they die;

you catch men that are dead

and bring them to life.

DAWSON TROTMAN

He said to them,
"Go into ALL THE WORLD
and PREACH the good news
to ALL CREATION."

MARK 16:15

God had an only Son
and He made Him a
missionary.

DAVID LIVINGSTONE

We are therefore
CHRIST'S AMBASSADORS,
as though God were making
his appeal through us.
We implore you on Christ's behalf:
BE RECONCILED TO GOD.

2 CORINTHIANS 5:20

CAN YOU SAY
THIS TO GOD?

I am not ashamed of the gospel,
because it is the power of God
for the salvation of everyone who believes:
first for the Jew, then for the Gentile.

ROMANS 1:16

Rise and shine, friend.
Everyone you meet today is on
HEAVEN'S MOST WANTED LIST.
CHARLES R. SWINDOLL

God wants to have a relationship
with all His children in
all His nations. We
must introduce
them to Him.
DAN AYRES

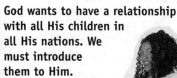

I pray
that you may be
ACTIVE
in **SHARING**
YOUR FAITH,
so that you
will have a full
understanding of
every good thing
we have
IN CHRIST.
PHILEMON 1:6

Stand up,
take a stand
for Jesus
till the whole
world sees us.
Following Him,
serving Him,
fighting the
fight that
we know
we will win.
BOB HARTMAN

The Bible tells us in Philemon 1:6 that we get to know Christ better the more we share Him.

God wants to use teens in His harvest. It's a big fat lie that we should be sheepish in sharing Christ with others.

There are so many ways to creatively witness. It's exciting to be used by God within your gifts and watch others learn to do the same.

Remember that you represent a mighty King who chooses to be reflected in you.

— DAVE DAVIDSON

HELL
isn't just for the weekend!

More people are alive today, and more souls are at stake, than the total number of people who have ever lived on the face of the earth in all of human history. This simply means that we can populate either Heaven or Hell by our obedience or our laziness. The world is going to hell on every continent! Is it God's fault that so few are hearing the Gospel — or is it the Church's?
KEITH GREEN

Crash Course
on God's Heart

What will you do that will **make an impact** on the world? What will you do that will **make a difference** in the lives of others for eternity? If you will not work to serve your fellow man, what will you do? The greatest gift that we can give to this world is **a life lived for Jesus.**

REBECCA ST. JAME

We've all seen them. Maybe you were one at some point. You know . . . the kids that never get picked for anything.

First the popular kids get picked, then the friends of the popular kids, then the kids that are good at that certain event. Then finally, they say "Okay, we'll take the guy that's left over." It hurts to get picked last.

It feels good to be picked first. To think that somebody thought enough of you to pick you first. You were their first round draft pick. There was no one else they would rather have on their team than you.

Jesus' famous last words were some of the most important you'll ever hear. Why? Because in His last words He picked you first.

As your leader and coach He gave you the best jersey on the team. Jesus said, "Go, make disciples, baptize and teach." And take note of what He said next, "And surely I am with you to the very end of the age."

He did not leave you on your own. He's right there with you today. Now it's your chance. Not to be a star, but to be a servant. Not to gain recognition for yourself, but to bring Him glory. Not to be prideful, but to be faithful. Not to gain treasures on earth, but treasures in heaven.

It's not a duty, it's a privilege. The coach is calling, but will you Go? The choice is up to you!

ERIC CHRISTENSEN

THERE IS
a living God.
He has spoken His word.
He means just what He says,
and will do all that He has
promised.

J. HUDSON TAYLOR

Outrageous & Contagious

Let us not become weary in
doing good, for at the proper time we
will reap a harvest if we do not give up.

GALATIANS 6:9

INSPIRE ME BIOGRAPHY™

BILLY GRAHAM, in 1944, became the first evangelist for the newly formed Youth For Christ, speaking at rallies in America and England. He had preached in person to over 110 million people by the early 1990's, more than anyone else in Christian history. Known as the "evangelist to the world," he was the first to utilize radio, television and satellite technology in evangelism.

The evangelistic harvest is always urgent.
The destiny of men and of nations
is always being decided.

BILLY GRAHAM

He called you
to this through our gospel,
that you might share
in the glory of our
Lord Jesus Christ.

2 THESSALONIANS 2:14

SOMEONE'S WAITING
to MEET JESUS
on the other side
OF YOUR FEAR.

CARMAN

THEREFORE, SINCE WE ARE SURROUNDED
BY SUCH A GREAT CLOUD OF WITNESSES,
LET US THROW OFF EVERYTHING THAT HINDERS
AND THE SIN THAT SO EASILY ENTANGLES,
AND LET US RUN WITH PERSEVERANCE
THE RACE MARKED OUT FOR US.

HEBREWS 12:1

an idea whose time has .com

For more stuff on evangelism and salvation check out

2Heaven.com

Your Online Referable Resource For Those

SEEKING GOD

Ministry
The Secret Of Falling In Love With Jesus Forever . . .
Honor Him Fearfully & Keep His Promises Faithfully

One of the best ways to share your faith is through action and by example. When we minister to others, we are fulfilling God's primary purpose for our lives.

Matthew 25:34-35 states, *"For I was hungry and you gave me something to eat, I was thirsty and you gave me something to drink, I was a stranger and you invited me in, I needed clothes and you clothed me, I was sick and you looked after me, I was in prison and you came to visit me."* Jesus later said, *"I tell you the truth, whatever you did for one of the least of these brothers of mine, you did for me."*

How does your life measure up in these outreach areas? Faith in action may be the best witness you will ever have.

E-MAIL (ETERNAL-MAIL) FROM JESUS

To: teens@8promises.com

I have chosen you to be a teenager now, the most exciting time to be alive in world history. You can help share the salvation truth of my love with everyone on earth.

Before I left earth I said, *"go and make disciples of all nations."* I am giving you the same mission today. Start with family and friends. Then, with the power of my Spirit, you can spread the gospel across the globe.

Your life is a living ministry that points others to me. Thank you for boldly sharing your faith.

Your Redeemer, Jesus

Think WOW Promise Plan™

Think WOW: Imagine if you were one of the diciples who heard the Great Commission straight from the lips of Jesus. You can be a bigger part of His kingdom. Think like Jesus and be His witness.

Make a VOW: Make a commitment today to do all you can to help carry out God's Great Commission. Always make it a top priority in your life. Make a promise to always let your light shine!

Plan HOW: Ask your youth pastor to help make a list of ministry opportunities in your community. Write down your personal goals for witnessing . Plan to invite some friends to church next week.

Do it NOW: Don't wait or procrastinate. Share your love of Jesus with at least three people today. The Bible tells us that "Now is the day of salvation." Seize the day God's way and don't delay!

Push the PLOW: Push the plow with persistent prayer. God's word tells us to pray for laborers because the harvest is ready! There are four ways to stay involved in missions work — PRAY, DO, GIVE, AND GO!

Keep this promise . . .

Image

I WILL BE
CONFIDENT IN CHRIST
Imitate Christ's Identity

*Be imitators of God, therefore, as dearly
loved children and live a life of love, just as
Christ loved us and gave himself up for us as
a fragrant offering and sacrifice to God.*
(Ephesians 5:1).

Who do you think you are? Do you have a high or low self-esteem? What effect does your self-worth have on your life?

We all must learn to receive God's love, while accepting ourselves and loving others. Relying on the self-talk of low self-esteem paralyzes our potential as a servant of God. Believing lies about our true identity can cause feelings of inferiority, inadequacy, and incompetence.

We must focus and fix our perspective (Hebrews 12:1,2) on the all-loving, all-perfect, all-powerful God. He embraces us as we are. God offers grace, mercy and peace even though we can't ever measure up to His standards.

Peers and even parents can throw messages of unworthiness at us. We must counteract with confidence in Christ and see ourselves as God does.

Nothing can separate you from the love of God. (Romans 8:38,39) You can always tell God your feelings. Never be afraid to express the real you to Jesus. You're sanctified in Him. He's the ultimate best friend! — DAVE DAVIDSON

Who, by the power that enables him
to bring everything under his control,
will transform our lowly
bodies so that they will be
like his glorious body

PHILIPPIANS 3:21

The pressure to conform . . .
    is even stronger than the need
for security and well being.
JAMES DOBSON

**For God did not give us
a spirit of timidity,**

BUT A SPIRIT OF POWER,
of love and of self-discipline.
2 TIMOTHY 1:7

(P)—
(R)—
(O)—
(M)—
(I)—
(S)—
(E)—
(S)—

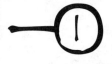

Image

Who You Are In Christ

Jesus died and rose for the real you, not for some phony persona. When you live with a fantasy or illusion of yourself, you miss out on fellowship with God.

God knows, loves, and sees the real you. With Jesus, just be yourself. Jesus wants to reach you, teach you, heal you, love you, embrace you, and spiritually change you so you can be the man or woman God intended.

God loves us, not because we make the grade on our own, but because we need His love. While we were yet sinners Christ died for us (Romans 5:8). He proved His love by demonstrating it. Good thing, because we need Jesus, for us to be righteous in God's sight, so we can fellowship with Him. — DAVE DAVIDSON

WHAT WE ARE is God's gift to us. WHAT WE BECOME is our gift to God.
LOUIS NIZER

We don't need "stuff" to be happy — the perfect body, or the best-looking car, the most up-to-date clothes, or the best house on the best street. We need Jesus Christ to be our total priority and not let that other stuff get in the way.

REBECCA ST. JAMES

Your perspective of yourself will determine the possibilities you pursue.
MIKE EVANS

Doing what is right isn't always popular, doing what is popular isn't always right.
ARGUS POSTER

In almost every case the beginning of new blessing is a new revelation of the character of God — more beautiful, more wonderful, more precious.
DR. J. ELDER CUMMING

WHAT??? Suppose that you are a prostitute.

One day you hear that the king has decreed that all prostitutes are forgiven. Since you're a prostitute, that's great news! But would it necessarily change your behavior or your self-perception? Probably not. You may dance in the streets for awhile, but chances are you would continue in your same vocation. You would see yourself as nothing more than a forgiven prostitute.

Now suppose the king not only forgave you, but he made you his bride as well. You're a queen. Would that change your behavior? Of course. Why would you want to live as a prostitute if you were a queen?

The church is the bride of Christ! You are far more likely to promote the kingdom if you are the queen rather than a forgiven prostitute. We are not redeemed caterpillars; we are butterflies. Why would you want to crawl in some false humility when you are called to mount up with wings as eagles?

NEIL ANDERSON

YOU ARE reconciled, regenerated and redeemed by God. You share in the destiny of Christ as a recipient of His eternal life. Condemnation has been removed by Christ's blood, shed on the cross. You are dead to sin, but alive to Christ. You are crucified with Christ, dead with Christ, buried with Christ and raised with Christ.

YOU ARE justified, forgiven and delivered. You are adopted and accepted into God's family and household. You are a citizen of heaven and are under the care of an all loving God. You are a gift from a merciful and compassionate God to Christ himself. You are an object of His love and grace for salvation and service.

YOU ARE also an object of His power, His faithfulness, His peace, His consolation, and His intercession. You possess God's inheritance by sharing the glory of Christ with all spiritual blessings in the heavenly realms.

YOU ARE united to the Father, Son and the Holy Spirit as a sheep in His flock, a part of His bride, a priest of the kingdom and as a saint.
You are born of the Spirit, baptized by the Spirit, indwelt by the Spirit, sealed by the Spirit, and
given spiritual gifts by the Spirit. As one of God's
chosen, holy and dearly loved, you have been given everything you need for life and godliness. You share in Christ's righteousness, election,
sonship, heirship, sanctification, priesthood, and kingship.

YOU ARE called to serve and love Him in an
abundant life presenting your body as a living sacrifice. You are God's worker, minister and ambassador to reach others with His love. You can
stand firm on the rock of salvation, a foundation that will never fail. You are never separated from
God's immense, awesome love. — DAVE DAVIDSON

Image

I must surrender my fascination
with myself to a more worthy
preoccupation with the
character and purposes of God.
I am not the point. He is. I exist
for Him. He does not exist for me.

LARRY CRABB

THE HARDEST THING TO HIDE IS SOMETHING THAT IS NOT THERE.
ERIC HOFFER

I thank God for my handicaps,
for through them I have found
myself, my work, and my God.
HELLEN KELLER

How great
is the
love the
Father has
lavished on
us, that we
should be
called
children
of God!
1 JOHN 3:1

Peace is full
confidence
that God is
who He
says He is
and that He
will keep
every
promise
in His Word.

DOROTHY
HARRISON
PENTECOST

In Your Face
G R A C E

When God asked Gideon to head up an Israelite
Army, Gideon said his family wasn't important and
he wasn't "good enough," but **God's Grace** showed
that His power enables leadership and victory,
leading Gideon and a selected army of only 300 to
win a mighty battle.

God chooses what we go through;
We choose how we go through it.
JOHN MAXWELL

The next time you pray, try picturing yourself as God does:
clothed in the righteousness of His Son and standing in
His presence. I guarantee your prayers will take on a new
reverence and a new meaning. Things have truly never
been the same since A.D. 33!
Bob Hartman

The great men and women of faith in Hebrews chapter 11 all were convinced that following God was absolutely worthwhile. They had a consuming passion for God.

Study the life of the apostle Paul and you will discover a man convinced of his true identity and citizenship in heaven. Paul said in Philippians 1:21, *"For me, to live is Christ."* This complete devotion can be your heart also.
— DAVE DAVIDSON

Understanding The Enemy

We must realize the devil is only a created being. Satan is not the opposite of God — he's not some evil, equal counterpart. God is all-powerful, all-knowing, and everywhere present. Satan is none of the above.
LOREN CUNNINGHAM

I WANT YOU TO KNOW . . . THAT THERE CAN AND SHOULD BE INCREASING VICTORY IN OUR OVERCOMING SIN, WHETHER IN "THOUGHT, WORD, OR DEED." JESUS CAME, DIED, AND ROSE AGAIN TO BREAK THE POWER OF SIN ONCE AND FOR ALL. BUT THE GRACE TO OVERCOME MUST FIRST BE APPLIED TO OUR MIND IF THE VICTORY IS TO SPREAD NATURALLY TO OUR ACTIONS.
DENNY GUNDERSON

Life's major pursuit is not knowing self . . . but knowing God . . . unless God is the major pursuit of our lives, all other pursuits are dead-end streets, including trying to know ourselves.
CHARLES R. SWINDOLL

OVER THE FENCE CONFIDENCE

Command and teach these things. Don't let anyone look down on you because you are young, but set an example for the believers in speech, in life, in love, in faith and in purity.
1 TIMOTHY 4:11,12

P R O M I S E S

I don't think of all the misery, but of all the beauty that still remains.
ANNE FRANK

God wisely designed the human body
so that we can neither pat our own backs
nor kick ourselves too easily.
ANONYMOUS

Do what you can,
with what you have,
with where you are.
THEODORE ROOSEVELT

*His divine power has given us everything
we need for life and godliness through our
knowledge of him who called us by his
own glory and goodness.*
2 PETER 1:3

Be strong
and courageous.
Do not be terrified; do not be discouraged,
for the LORD your God will be with you
wherever you go.   JOSHUA 1:8,9

CAN YOU SAY THIS TO GOD?
But one thing I do: Forgetting
what is behind and straining
toward what is ahead, I press
on toward the goal to win the
prize for which God has called
me heavenward in
Christ Jesus.
PHILIPPIANS 3:13-14

One man with courage
makes a majority.
Andrew Jackson

You're running a risk
whenever you're not running a risk.
For every risk you take
prepares you for the next risk you take.
DAVE DAVIDSON

The "W A W O P T" SYNDROME

Many teens and even adults have been known to suffer from a chronic condition known as W A W O P T syndrome.

It often strikes victims in public places. At times it can come on suddenly with a gripping fear, when teens are sitting quietly alone at home.

The W A W O P T syndrome is an acronym for **"Worried About What Other People Think."**

This paralyzing condition can include worry about your physical size and shape, the clothes you wear and whether you are popular or not. Some worry about what others think of their parents, brothers and sisters, the street they live on, the church they attend, and whether anyone noticed new overnight zits.

The only known antidote for W A W O P T syndrome is to totally identify your self-image with Jesus, and know that you are a child of God, the Creator of the universe.

This treatment can result in immediate relief of symptoms and can create a renewed confidence in Christ and a joyful and peaceful heart. — DAN DAVIDSON

God made you as you are in order to use you as He planned.
S.C. MCAULEY

CAN YOU SAY THIS TO GOD?

I have been crucified with Christ
and I no longer live,
but Christ lives in me.
The life I live in the body,
I live by faith in the Son of God,
who loved me and gave himself up for me.
GALATIANS 2:20

WE TRUST JESUS WITH THE PAST, THE PRESENT AND THE FUTURE BECAUSE **HE IS THE SAME YESTERDAY, TODAY AND FOREVER.**
DAVE DAVIDSON

THEREFORE, SINCE WE HAVE SUCH A HOPE, WE ARE VERY BOLD.
2 CORINTHIANS 3:12

Image
The Secret Of Falling In Love With Jesus Forever . . .
Honor Him Fearfully & Keep His Promises Faithfully

Now all has been heard; here is the conclusion of the matter: Fear God and keep His commandments, for this is the whole duty of man (Ecclesiastes 12:13).

The Bible tells us that we are fearfully and wonderfully made, created by God himself and made in His image. Our self-image should be based on the image of God!

Ephesians 2:10 says, *"For we are God's workmanship, created in Christ Jesus to do good works, which God prepared in advance for us to do."*

God is the master builder of our self-image. Since He created the original blueprint, give the building permit back to Him. He has some awesome future plans for your life.

E-MAIL (ETERNAL-MAIL) FROM JESUS

To: teens@8promises.com

I want you to know that you come from a royal family — my Father adopted you into His kingdom. No matter what anyone else says, you are a child of the King!

Look to me and lean on me throughout the day. All things are possible through me. I will give you strength to accomplish my will in your life.

Always be confident in my name. I will never leave your side. I will always be there to love you and to lead you.

Your Creator, Jesus

Think WOW Promise Plan™

Think WOW: What if you were made in the image of the Creator of the universe. Well you are! Think about how awesome that is. You are part of His royal family, a citizen of heaven.

Make a VOW: Make a commitment to stay in the family of God. Claim your heavenly heritage and become a wholehearted devoted servant of God. He is ready to use you in mighty ways for His glory.

Plan NOW - Write down areas of your life in which you lack confidence. Make a plan to read God's Word and pray daily to discover the truth about who you are in the Lord.

Do it NOW: You are a child of God today. Don't wait until the future to enjoy godly blessings in your life. Thank God right now for saving you from sin. You can be confident in Christ!

Push the PLOW: It can be hard to stay confident everyday. Others may try and cut you down but keep your life planted in Jesus. Pray for patience and perseverance from the Holy Spirit.

Keep this promise . . .

Sex

I WILL SAVE SEX FOR MARRIAGE
Demonstrate Purity

*Since we have these promises, dear friends,
let us purify ourselves from everything that
contaminates body and spirit, perfecting holiness
out of reverence for God
(2 Corinthians 7:1).*

Welcome to the first chapter. Admit it. Didn't you sneak a peak at this chapter first? Sex is a timely topic with teens. Hopefully you're not looking for a loophole but ready to find out how it's possible to glorify God with your sex drive.

You already know everything you need to know about the basics of sex for now. God's plan for sex is to save it for marriage.

In this romantic and sensual world it seems that almost anything goes. You can choose to follow God's plan and not the world's. The risks and rewards run high as intense images, emotions, and opinions affect relationships.

The right love song performed at the right time can stir the heart like a blender or crash it like a dented fender. What you need to know about sex is how amazing it is to WAIT for God's best plan.

In Romans 13:13-14, God's Word urges and advises us to behave decently and to literally clothe ourselves with the Lord Jesus Christ instead of gratifying sinful desires. You have to dress the part in your heart.

— DAVE DAVIDSON

Do you not know that
your body
is a temple
of the Holy Spirit,
who is in you, whom you have
received from God? You are not
your own; you were bought at a
price. Therefore honor God
with your body.
1 Corinthians 6:19-20

(P)—
(R)—
(O)—
(M)—
(I)—
(S)—
(E)—
(S)—

Today's teens are under a lot of pressure and are being forced to make a lot of big decisions early in life — especially when it comes to sexuality. I am a virgin, and I'm proud of it. I've made that commitment to God and to my future husband — whoever that may be.

REBECCA ST. JAMES

S

Love is not an emptiness
longing to be filled —
it is a fullness
pressing to be released.
J. KENNEDY SHULTZ

THE BEST SEX, EVER!

Great sex is like a spectacular Fourth of July fireworks show. What makes a fireworks display fantastic is proper timing.

God created sex in much the same way. He planned it in His perfect timing, for our enjoyment. God's timing for sex is always within marriage, between husband and wife.

Saving sex for marriage allows for a spectacular grand finale, with many encore performances.

— DAN DAVIDSON

Forced love is never genuine,
so commit your heart to prayer
and patience.
BECCA LYNN

But you, man of God, flee from all this,
and pursue righteousness, godliness, faith, love,
endurance and gentleness.
Fight the good fight of the faith.
Take hold of the eternal life to which you were
called when you made your good confession
in the presence of many witnesses.
1 TIMOTHY 6:11-12

CAN YOU SAY THIS TO GOD?

Put to death, therefore, whatever belongs to your earthly nature: sexual immorality, impurity, lust, evil desires and greed, which is idolatry.
COLOSSIANS 3:5

In Your Face GRACE

King David really messed up when his eyes wandered from the balcony and he spied Bathsheba, resulting in adultery and the arrangement of her husband's death, but **God's Grace** ministered to David and he became a godly King that was very close to the heart of God.

LOVE IS AN IRRESISTIBLE DESIRE TO BE IRRESISTIBLY DESIRED.
ROBERT FROST

STRAIGHT TALK ➤

FOR GIRLS ONLY:

TO ALL TEENAGE GIRLS: One of the MOST IMPORTANT things to keep in mind about dating, sex, and relationships is **"NEVER UNDERESTIMATE THE POTENTIAL OF A TEENAGE BOY'S SEXUALITY."**

Sure he can be honest, cute, and a Christian, but he is turned on faster, stronger, and easier than you are sexually. Any efforts to tease, flirt, and test affections may have you saying "sorry" to yourself and to God for not guarding your heart. Never take for granted this secret warning.

Don't think you can really know or anticipate someone's sexual urges, preferences, or opinions just because you know them as a friend.

Even though the guy you're attracted to is suave and handsome, in one way or another he is likely to be struggling with self-image, social pressure, and sexual issues.

Guys do not need extra curricular encouragement from fashion or passion to notice your body. Girls, be yourself, but prayerfully consider dressing more modestly despite the latest trends.

This is not to demean or discourage the teen male who is also reading this "Girls Only" section. Face it guys, you need girls to know that you may be weak and vulnerable, not for the devil's foot hold, but for victory in Christ.

On one hand, no guy wants you to know he is vulnerable and on the other hand every guy wishes to be better understood, but be careful sharing information about such struggles. There is a time and place for exposing secrets of the heart. — DAVE DAVIDSON

**Dear friends,
I urge you, as aliens
and strangers in the world,
to abstain from sinful desires,
which war against your soul.**
1 PETER 2:11

I was pursuing something when I wasn't ready to be committed. I was wasting my time and hurting people.

Nowadays, you go out with someone, break up, and move on to the next person. But there's always this part of you you're holding back because you know what it's like to be hurt. It would be wonderful if, when a person gets married, they haven't gone through eight boyfriends. They give everything because their heart hasn't been chipped away.
JOSHUA HARRIS

Leaving Lust in the Dust

When tempted, no one should say, "God is tempting me."
For God cannot be tempted by evil, nor does He tempt
anyone; but each one is tempted when, by his own evil
desire, he is dragged away and enticed. Then, after desire
has conceived, it gives birth to sin; and sin, when it is
full-grown, gives birth to death.
JAMES 1:13-17

Though temptation itself isn't sin, stopping to survey and study the situation plants the seed of sin in our heart.

We are enticed by our own lust. Lust is a strong desire that is often coupled with forbidden longings and precarious cravings. Satan is smart enough to tempt us in areas where we may be vulnerable. Satan isn't a creator like God. Instead, Satan takes what God has created for good and twists it with perversion.

Temptation can be greater when strong desires have become ungodly evil footholds in our life. This can be caused by unresolved sin allowing the enemy a clearer target on which to fire his darts of deception.

Within the trial, test, and turmoil of temptation, God gives us a guarantee. He always provides a way of escape. 1 Corinthians 10:13 provides the biblical evidence that God is standing by ready to rescue you from falling into sin.

We need to take authority over the devil and claim God's victory by fleeing temptation and pursuing righteousness. (1 Timothy 6:11; 2 Timothy 2:22)

You can't flee from a sinful foothold still planted in your mind. Instead, replace sensual thoughts, vulnerable attitudes, and alluring images with whatever is true, noble, right, pure, lovely, admirable, excellent, or praiseworthy. (Philippians 4:8)

By claiming a Bible verse, singing a chorus, or offering a spontaneous prayer of thankfulness, you can get your head in gear and your heart in purity.

— DAVE DAVIDSON

No temptation has seized you
except what is common to man.
And God is faithful; he will not
let you be tempted beyond
what you can bear. But when
you are tempted, he will also
provide a way out so that you can
stand up under it.
1 CORINTHIANS 10:13

Living Below The Balcony

Where do you hang out when it comes to sexual desires? King David spent more time than he should have out on a balcony that overlooked Bathsheba's bathing room.

2 Samuel 11:2 describes the situation, *"One evening David got up from his bed and walked around on the roof of the palace. From the roof he saw a woman bathing. The woman was very beautiful . . . "*

The rest of story . . . David gave in to temptation in a big way. It was the King's actions that put him in a place of temptation to begin with. He "got up" and he "walked around" and then he "saw" a woman bathing. As George Verwer puts it, " David should have repented upon the roof, not a year later; he reached a stage that no believer should have to reach, where he had to be called forth and publicly rebuked."

God's Word assures us that He will always provide a way of escape when temptation is near. (1 Corinthians 10:13) However, if we get up and walk around and look for temptation, we may end up far away from God's emergency escape hatch.

Sometimes it's best to just stay put. Be more like Joseph who chose victory in a tempting situation. Where you decide to hang out greatly affects your daily walk of purity in the eyes of Jesus. — DAN DAVIDSON

CAN YOU SAY THIS TO GOD?

I really believe if we're going to be serious about living sold-out for God, we need to say, "I do not want to fill my mind with the junk that's out there. I don't want to waste my time putting things into my brain that I won't be able to get out."
REBECCA ST. JAMES

HYPOCRITE: SOMEONE WHO COMPLAINS THAT THERE'S TOO MUCH SEX AND VIOLENCE ON HIS VCR.
ANONYMOUS

THIS Is What LOVE Is . . .

Love is patient, love is kind. It does not envy, it does not boast, it is not proud. Love is not rude, is not self seeking, it is not easily angered, it keeps no record of wrongs. Love does not delight in evil but rejoices in truth. It always protects, always trusts, always hopes, always perseveres.
1 CORINTHIANS 13:5

P R O M I S E S

Love must be
SINCERE.
ROMANS 12:9

LOVE is that condition in which
the happiness of another person
is essential to your own joy.
GEORGE ELIOT

I make it a rule of
Christian duty
never to go to a
place where
there is not
room for my
Master as well
as myself.
JOHN NEWTON

The deepest pleasures
in life don't satisfy
— they point us
forward. Until we
attain unity with
Christ in heaven,
an inconsolable
longing for more
will remain in every
human heart.
LARRY CRABB

You can GIVE
without LOVING,
but you can never
LOVE without
GIVING.
UNKNOWN

The Lord knows
the thoughts of man.
PSALM 94:11

AVOID circumstances where compromise is likely.
. . . Sexual contact between a boy and a
girl is a progressive thing. In other worlds, the amount of
touching, caressing, and kissing that occurs in the early
days tends to increase as they become more familiar and
at ease with one another. Likewise, the amount of contact
necessary to excite one another increases day by day,
leading in many cases to the ultimate act of sin and its
inevitable consequence.

This progression must be consciously resisted by
Christian young people who want to serve God and live by
His standards. They can resist this trend by placing delib-
erate controls on the physical aspect of their relationship
right from the first date.
JAMES DOBSON

The Fashion
Of Passion

ADMIT ONE

985003 · 985003

©W.I. Rogers Company

> I USED TO CHECK OFF
> MY LIST TO SEE
> WHAT I MISSED . . .
> LOOKING FOR HEARTS
> OFF A GROCERY LIST.
> I'M NOT TOO SURE WHAT
> LOVE IS ANYMORE.
> MATT MALYON

Sometimes we can approach love like buying groceries. We check off attractive attributes and items we wish for while shopping for what we think is best for us.

As we walk down the aisle the world entices us into seductions we never intended to even look at. In a scantily dressed sexy world, we can either pursue the world's fashion of passion or guard our hearts and pursue a passionate path of purity.

Whose definition of love and passion will you endorse as your own? Whose romantic worldview will you see love through? Will you choose God's Word or the latest loose lie from the devil?

Understanding the intricacies of a relationship is like trying to find and thread a needle in a haystack during a hayride. It's a bumpy ride on a fast track that requires precision.

Every friendship and dating situation ultimately prepares you for your future potential marriage. Ask yourself "What can I learn about handling my emotions in this situation? How can God use my latest feelings of disappointment or joy to prepare me to be a great spouse someday?"

Every broken heart comes with a secret message that can build you up and encourage you. (Romans 8:28) Can you come to the point in heart to say . . . "When I love without reward, without connection, without regard for my affections . . . this is when the refining begins melting motives into purity."

— DAVE DAVIDSON

**A man in passion
rides a horse that
runs away with him.**
C.H. SPURGEON

HONOR ONE ANOTHER
ABOVE YOURSELVES.
ROMANS 12:10

(P)—
(R)—
(O)—
(M)—
(I)—
(S)—
(E)—
(S)—

Sex
The Secret Of Falling In Love With Jesus Forever . . .
Honor Him Fearfully & Keep His Promises Faithfully

Remember that God created sex. The world didn't. The devil didn't. God's plan for sex is always within the sacred relationship of marriage between a husband and wife.

While you're waiting as a teen, supreme balance is required when aiming your passions toward one another. It is delicately dangerous, like tightrope walking over Niagara Falls.

When God says "NO," it means He wants to protect, preserve, and prepare us for something better. It means a more fulfilling "YES," is waiting right just around the corner.

Create in me a PURE heart, O God, and renew a steadfast spirit within me.
PSALMS 51:10

E-MAIL (ETERNAL-MAIL) FROM JESUS

To: teens@8promises.com

You have many choices in life. The decisions about relation ships that you make each day are very important to your future. It all comes down to this personal promise, "I will save sexual love for marriage."

I have prepared a path of holiness for you. Read the Song of Solomon in my Word to get a glimpse of godly love within marriage.

You were created with emotion and desires. If you follow my path of purity, you will experience great blessings in your life.

Your Protector, Jesus

Think WOW Promise Plan™

Think WOW: What if you waited for sex until marriage? What if you preserved your purity for your future spouse? You can receive the abundant blessings God has planned for your life.

Make a VOW: Maintaining sexual purity requires a strong commitment. Make a pledge to yourself, to God, and your future spouse to remain holy in all aspects of relationships before marriage.

Plan NOW: Create a plan for self-control and holiness. Write down specific ideas to eliminate tempting situations. Stay plugged into God's Word to learn more about His will for your love life.

Do it NOW: Don't do sex now! It doesn't matter if others are doing it. You can choose to remain faithful with a purity promise before God. Set an example today for your friends.

Push the PLOW: Because of strong desires and emotions, it can be challenging to wait for sex. Be diligent. Never give in to feelings. Pray for the Holy Spirit to guide you with the fruit of self-control.

Keep this promise . . .

Eternity

I WILL MEASURE
MY LIFE.
Evaluate your life story.

*Now all has been heard; here is the conclusion of the
matter: Fear God and keep His commandments,
for this is the whole duty of man*
(Ecclesiates 12:13).

Measuring your life and maintaining an eternal
perspective affects all the other promises you make, break
and keep in life.

Many people tried to make a mark while on
earth — to reach the top, to climb the ladder of success,
money, and fame. However, the things of the world will be
gone in the blink of an eye.

D. L. Moody once said, "Seeking to perpetuate
one's name on earth is like writing on the sand by the
seashore; to be perpetual it must be written on the
eternal shores."

Just like compound interest in a bank account,
the earlier you start investing in eternity, the greater the
return. You are writing your life story everyday. Make sure
the final chapter is in heaven.

You have your whole life ahead of you. You
don't know how long you will live, so live wisely.
Psalm 90:10,12 says, *"The length of our days is seventy
years — or eighty, if we have the strength; yet their span
is but trouble and sorrow, for they quickly pass, and we fly
away. . . . Teach us to number our days aright, that we
may gain a heart of wisdom."*

Measure your life everyday with the perspective
of this poem, "This day too soon will pass, only what's
done for Christ will last."   — DAN & DAVE DAVIDSON

(P)—

(R)—

(O)—

(M)—

(I)—

(S)—

(E)—

(S)—

You know, we'll hardly get our feet out of
time into eternity that we'll bow our heads
in shame and humiliation. We'll gaze on
eternity and say, "Look at all the riches there
were in Jesus Christ, and I've come to the
Judgment Seat almost a pauper."
A.W. TOZER

CAN YOU SAY THIS TO GOD?

God has not called me to be successful;
He has called me to be faithful.
MOTHER TERESA

A LIFE STORY
INVENTORY™

Picture yourself sitting on a rocking chair in the shade,
With writing pen and paper, sipping lemonade.

LOOK AHEAD

Imagine your last days on earth;
Measure in your mind your life's worth.

WRITE DOWN EACH WISH

Replay your life, record and reflect
Each wish, dream, reward and regret.

SEND IT BACK IN TIME

Take the memo in your mind
And send it back in time.

LIVE THE LIST

Begin to live your life the way
You'd live it again, starting today.

If I Could Live My Life Again

I wouldn't let my heart regret.

I'd do my dream to the extreme.

I wouldn't skip praise and worship.

I'd lay up treasure in heavenly measure.

I'd find a way to say "I love you every day."

I'd witness and share in word, deed and prayer.

I'd make prayer more a part of my life from the start.

I wouldn't be the type to grumble, groan or gripe.

I wouldn't devote my soul to the remote control.

I'd have integrity even when others couldn't see.

I'd repeat less rumor and spread more humor.

I wouldn't always go with the status quo.

I'd be a trailblazer and a people praiser.

I'd realize my pride is often too wide.

I'd be content and quick to repent.

I'd be strong to admit my wrong.

I'd keep in mind the finish line.

**I'VE THOUGHT ABOUT MANY THINGS,
BUT THE MOST AWESOME, THE MOST TERRIFYING,
THE MOST SHATTERING THOUGHT I'VE EVER HAD,
IS MY PERSONAL ACCOUNTABILITY TO GOD ONE DAY.**

*I have come that they may
have life, and have it to the fullest.*
JOHN 10:10

No matter how wonderful your understanding of God is, you have never begun even to realize how good God is. . . . It is a tremendous joy to God that you and others who love him will be able to share with Him all that His love is planning for you forever and ever and ever!

He is so delighted, so thrilled, so expectant. He has only given you hints of all the delightful surprises He is planning . . . It will take you all of eternity to experience all God is planning for you.

The question is, will it be only existence? Or, will it be life in the fullest, most wonderful sense of the term. It is not merely a question of heaven or hell. It is a question of all that heaven can include for you. More than you have realized, your future reward is in your hands.

WESLEY DUEWEL

No one really knows why they're alive until they know what they'd die for.

MARTIN LUTHER KING JR.

THE MOST IMPORTANT DAY OF YOUR LIFE

Just imagine if one day of school would determine your final grade for all your twelve years of academic study. Your permanent school record would hinge on one 24-hour span of your life.

Wouldn't you want to know which day it was going to be? The preparation for that day would be like no other day in your life, considering the weight it would carry for your future.

In a similar way, there is one day in your life that holds great significance in light of eternity. It is the day you accept Jesus as your personal Saviour. On that day the angels rejoice because your heavenly address is verified!

Your life on earth will affect your position and rewards forever. Once you are "born again" into His Kingdom, God stands by ready to reveal His perfect will to you in His perfect timing.

Like a vine in John 15, all you have to do is be faithful and He will be fruitful. *"Let us hold unswervingly to the hope we profess, for he who promised is faithful"* (Hebrews 10:23). As George Verwer says, "Once we begin to really obey God and hence see fruit in our lives, then we gain a greater assurance."

If you haven't yet asked Jesus to come into your heart, do it today. It will be the most important day of your life. As God's Word says, *"Today is the day of salvation."*

— DAN & DAVE DAVIDSON

He is no fool
who gives what he cannot keep to gain what he cannot lose.
JIM ELLIOT

**Am I trying to win
the approval of men, or of God?
Or am I trying to please men?
If I were still trying to please men,
I would not be a servant of Christ.**
GALATIANS 1:10

GOD'S ETERNAL JOURNAL™

Benjamin Disraeli once said, "youth is a blunder; manhood a struggle; old age a regret."

You can choose to rewrite a new quote with your life, "Youth is full of hope in Christ; manhood is a journey of God's grace; old age a foreshadowing of eternal rewards in heaven."

You are writing your own autobiography every day of your life. The sooner you realize that you will someday die, the sooner you can really start living today as a devoted servant of Jesus.

God is also keeping an account of your life in His Eternal Journal. You cannot hide any action, thought or word from God. He sees every hidden thing. What do you think God wrote in His Eternal Journal about your life yesterday, last week, last year?

Your complete earthly biography will be revealed on judgement day. God is measuring every second of your life. Don't you think you should start measuring your life too? — Dan & Dave Davidson

But store up for yourselves treasures in heaven, where moth and rust do not destroy, and where thieves do not break in and steal.
MATTHEW 6:20

Live to the hilt every situation you believe to be the will of God.
JIM ELLIOTT

INSPIRE ME BIOGRAPHY™

ERIC LIDDELL not only measured his life one day at a time in light of eternity, but also had a great respect for the Sabbath. At the Paris Olympic games in 1924, his Christian convictions led him to turn down competitive heats in the 100 meters, which were held on Sunday, an event in which he was expected to win the gold medal. A few days later he did win a gold medal in record breaking time in the 400 meters in which he was inexperienced. The next year he went to China as a missionary.

MAKE YOUR PLANS
AS FANTASTIC AS YOU LIKE,
because 25 years from now, they will seem mediocre.
MAKE YOUR PLANS
**10 TIMES AS GREAT
AS YOU FIRST PLANNED,**
and 25 years from now you will wonder why you
did not make them 50 times as great.

HENRY CURTIS

We don't have the luxury of
making life decisions without
consulting the One who has
ordered our lives! Be alert and
seek God. Bring your life
before Him and allow it to
be tested by His Holy Spirit.

MELODY GREEN SIEVRIGHT

In Your Face
G R A C E

The prodigal son lived for the pleasures of today,
failing to measure his life in light of eternity,
but **God's Grace** was shown to him through his
loving father who forgave him and welcomed him
back into his family.

**Never be afraid
to trust
an unknown future
to an all-knowing God.**

CORRIE TEN BOOM

SNAP YOUR FINGERS,
BLINK YOUR EYES ...
THAT'S HOW MUCH YOUR TIME
ON EARTH CAN BE COMPARED
TO ETERNITY. ARE YOU
LIVING FOR THE SNAP
AND THE BLINK OF LIFE
OR FOR THE FOREVER
OF YOUR FUTURE?

DAN DAVIDSON

(P) — (R) — (O) — (M) — (I) — (S) — (E) — (S)

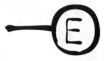

Citizenship In Heaven

But our citizenship is in heaven . . .
And we eagerly await a Saviour
from there, the Lord Jesus Christ.
PHILIPPIANS 3:20

It's fascinating that the most important, most strategic, most enduring place in the universe gets so little attention. The moon and Mars get more press than heaven. Yet heaven is of unrivaled significance. When we stretch our view of life to embrace its reality, all of life is wonderfully rearranged.

Eternity is primary. Heaven must become our first and ultimate point of reference. We are built for it, redeemed for it, and on our way to it. All that we have, are, and accumulate must be seen as resources by which we can influence and impact the world beyond. Even our tragedies are viewed as events that can bring eternal gain.

Hope in eternity is founded in the reality of an empty tomb — in the supernatural revelations to the apostle John that unfold for us in the book of Revelation.
JOSEPH STOWELL

REGRET
is an appalling waste of energy;
you can't build on it;
it's only good for wallowing in.
KATHRYN MANSFIELD

EVERY DAY THAT PASSES IS ONE DAY CLOSER TO CHRIST'S RETURN.
DAN DAVIDSON

CAN YOU SAY THIS TO GOD?

I will place no value on anything I have or may
possess except in relation to the kingdom of Christ.
If anything will advance the interests of that kingdom,
it shall be given or kept only as by giving or keeping it
I may advance the glory of Him to whom I owe all my
hopes for time and eternity.

DAVID LIVINGSTON

AS LONG AS YOU ARE LIVING, AS LONG AS YOU
ARE AWAKE, HAVE BOTH
EYES PEELED OPEN.
HAVE EACH HAND
REACHING OUT READY
TO EXPERIENCE
WHATEVER COMES YOUR
WAY. KEEP YOUR MIND
ALERT WITH WISDOM AND
YOUR HEART OPEN WITH LOVE AND AS MUCH
AS POSSIBLE, LIVE LIFE TO THE FULLEST.

DAVE DAVIDSON

**Why, you do not
even know what
will happen
tomorrow.**

WHAT IS YOUR LIFE?

**You are a mist
that appears
for a little while
and then
vanishes.**

JAMES 4:14

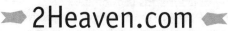

Eternity
The Secret Of Falling In Love With Jesus Forever . . .

Honor Him Fearfully &
Keep His Promises Faithfully

When you are in the habit of reflecting on eternity and how your life fits God's plan, all other aspects of your spiritual life come into focus. Suddenly your priorities are rearranged with a heavenly perspective.

Wesley Duewel once said, "Your daily choices have eternal consequences, and God does not choose for you. You yourself must choose wisely."

Time is short and life is precious. We must ask ourselves, how much eternity is in what we're doing today.

The fear of the Lord adds length to life, but the years of the wicked are cut short.
PROVERBS 10:27

E-MAIL (ETERNAL-MAIL) FROM JESUS

To: teens@8promises.com

Someday in the future I will measure your life to determine your heavenly rewards. It will be like a test of fire where all the sin, and every worthless thought and deed will be burned up like wood, hay, and straw.

All your godly actions, pure thoughts, and promises kept will survive like gold, silver and precious stones. Then I will give out my heavenly prizes!

I am also preparing a place for you in heaven so you and I can share an eternity of joy and fellowship together.

Your Redeemer, Jesus

Think WOW Promise Plan™

Think WOW: Think about the "crown of right-eousness" that God promises us when we persevere for His glory. Heaven is going to be more awesome than we could ever imagine.

Make a VOW: Be devoted in your focus on eternity. Despite setbacks in life, trials and persecution, maintain confidence in Christ. It is only through Him that we have the power to persevere.

Plan HOW: Make a list of rewards and regrets you might have at the end of your life. TAKE A LIFE STORY INVENTORY™ and begin to live the life you'd live if you could live again, starting today.

Do It NOW: Build your life on the foundation of Jesus Christ, the chief Cornerstone and Rock of our salvation! Measure everything you do today with God's eternal journal, His book of life.

Push the PLOW: Keep an eternal perspective as you follow God's commandments. Always keep His promises, persevere, and remember to keep your eyes on God's prize.

Keep this promise . . .

Scripture

I WILL GROW
IN GOD'S WORD.
Activate faith.

All scripture is God-breathed and is useful for teaching, rebuking, correcting and training in righteousness, so that the man of God may be thoroughly equipped for every good work (2 Timothy 3:16).

The Bible, inspired by God himself, is filled with His fulfilled promises. He is the King and sovereign Lord over all of time and your future. The Bible is God's love letter to us.

God's Word analyzes motives, rearranges purpose, and corrects wrongs. It pierces pride, encourages hope, restores faith, and sustains joy. The Word confronts with conviction, reveals with relevance, and exposes selfishness.

The Bible arouses the apathetic, prods the seeking, and guides the lost. It exposes illusions, uncovers wickedness, and unveils truth. It helps heal the hurting by providing comfort and confidence. Bible verses can be intelligently intriguing and creatively challenging, but also have the power to change lives and excite the heart like a lightning bolt.

The Bible is the solid-rock Word of the Living God! His Word remains unchangeable. It is always up-to-date and applicable to your life.

Whether it burns like Jeremiah's bones (Jeremiah 20:9), whispers like Elijah's still small voice (1 Kings 19:12), or decodes wisdom like Daniel's dreams, the Bible still speaks to us today. It's an intimate face-to-face communion much like Moses and God spoke as friends. (Exodus 33:11)

It offers honesty, authority and power. God's Word calls us into compassion, spurs us into service and delivers us from darkness. It awakens worship, sparks the Spirit, and generously gives out grace.

The Bible is relevant because Jesus is Lord, the author, and finisher of our faith.

— DAVE DAVIDSON

You cannot believe anything until you accept it as genuine and put it to the test of experience, and this is true of the Word.

RAY C. STEDMAN

W.O.W.
Wondered On the Word

The next time you read your Bible, pause before you open it. Think about the fact that God, the creator of the universe, has left a written revelation of His love for you. WOW!

When was the last time you have thought WOW about a Bible passage? Have you ever read a Bible verse and been taken aback by its truth and revelation? Have you ever felt an interesting insight leap off the page right into your heart?

Thinking "WOW" is being "Wondered On the Word." It's looking to a verse by faith with the expectation that heavenly truths will bless and transform your heart.

Sometimes a verse can be best understood or remembered in its nutshell form. When it's put in a different light, the truth multiplies like light shining through a prism, making its brilliance more visible.

Thinking and reacting in a "WOW" mindset prepares your heart to accept God's love and truth.

C.L.I.C.K.
Christ's Life Is Commitment Key

After the "WOW" it's time for the love of Christ to "CLICK" in your heart, mind, and soul. The book of John tells us how awesome the Word of God is. Galatians 2:20 explains our identity with Christ. His life has been exchanged for ours. Chapters 6-8 in Romans explain even more about our life in Christ. In fact, the entire Bible can be described as a key to living for, and more like, Christ.

In basketball the crowd may be in awe and think "WOW" at a long three point attempt, but the cheers come when the ball goes through the basket. Being wondered on the Word catches your attention, but a "CLICK" (Christ's Love Is Commitment Key) is when the basket is made and points are registered on the scoreboard.

Bible verses start to "Click" when you compare and concentrate on the truth with the life. Jesus is the way, the truth, and the life (John 14:6). Jesus wants for us to make a connection between the written living Word and our daily Christian walk. The Holy Spirit helps to transform our nature by the renewing of our minds. (Romans 12:1,2)

Z.A.P.
Zealously Applying Principle

"Zap" is where the rubber hits the road and scripture is applied in our lives. It's a living rehearsal of a Bible verse. A "Zap" (Zealously Applying Principle) is the lightning bolt that shakes the earth with a power beam of light from heaven.

Biblical truths energize our walk with Jesus. "Verse Rehearse" is making God's Word your life story by rehearsing the wonderful principles found in Christ's life in the Bible. Wow, Click, Zap!

Zap is the faithful action step. The "Wow, Click, Zap" approach is a Bible study method that you can use anytime you read the Bible. The meanings behind these acronyms can help you create a habit of living out God's Word. — DAN & DAVE DAVIDSON

KEEP THIS EASY-TO-REMEMBER ACRONYM OUTLINE IN MIND TO KNOW WHAT TYPE OF TREASURES TO LOOK FOR WHEN READING THE BIBLE.

Attitude to change.

Promise to claim.

Prayer to pray.

Lesson to learn.

Yielding from temptation.

Sin to confess.

Command to obey.

Reason to thank God.

Indication of God's Character.

Principle to remember.

Truth to believe.

Understanding to discern.

Right to repeat.

Example to follow.

Blessed are those who hunger and thirst for righteousness, for they will be filled. But seek first his kingdom and his righteousness, and all these things will be given to you as well.
MATTHEW 5:6; 6:33

THE GOOD BOOK

If there's one thing the Bible dares to do that no other book in the world does, it's to accurately predict the future. God can arrange the situations and circumstances of history to bring about patterns laid down before the foundation of the world. The outline of many of these patterns is revealed in the Bible.

There are about 3,856 verses directly or indirectly concerned with prophecy in Scripture — about one verse in six tells of future events! God's challenge to the world is "Prove Me now — I am the Lord . . . I will speak, and the word that I speak shall come to pass." (See Jeremiah 28:9; Ezekiel 12:25, 24:14) Buddhists, Confucianists, and Muslims have their own sacred writings, but in them the element of prophecy is obviously absent.

In the brief life of Jesus alone we see over 300 fulfilled prophecies. The odds that these would all coincide by accident in one person are laughable. By the laws of chance, the conservative odds of even just 48 of those prophecies being fulfilled by one man are one in 10^{157}. (That's 1 followed by 157 zeros!!!)

1,000,000,000,000,000,000,000,000,000,000,
000,000,000,000,000,000,000,000,000,000,000,
000,000,000,000,000,000,000,000,000,000,000,
000,000,000,000,000,000,000,000,000,000,000,
000,000,000,000,000,000,000,000,000

Let me try to give you an idea of how immense this number is. We'll take a very small object, let's say an electron. (Electrons are so small that if you lined them up, it would take 2-1/2 quadrillion of them to equal one inch.) If you tried to put this many electrons into a big pile, it would be 10,000,000,000 times larger than the universe as we know it — which scientists calculate to be 6,000,000,000 light-years across. (A light-year is the distance that light willl travel in one year, moving at the speed of 186,000 miles per second.)

Now, take just one electron out and color it red. Stir it back into this pile for a hundred thousand years with all the others. Then blindfold a man and send him in to pick it out — first time! Impossible? These would be the same odds that one man would live and die according to only 48 of the prophecies about the Messiah, if it were only an accident.

The Scriptures specifically predict events and happenings that are as modern as tomorrow's news release.

WINKIE PRATNEY

**The grass withers
and the flowers fall,
but the word of our God
stands forever.**
ISAIAH 40:8

DO NOT LET THIS BOOK OF THE LAW DEPART FROM YOUR MOUTH; MEDITATE ON IT DAY AND NIGHT, SO THAT YOU MAY BE CAREFUL TO DO EVERYTHING WRITTEN IN IT. THEN YOU WILL BE PROSPEROUS AND SUCCESSFUL. HAVE I NOT COMMANDED YOU? BE STRONG AND COURAGEOUS. DO NOT BE TERRIFIED; DO NOT BE DISCOURAGED, FOR THE LORD YOUR GOD WILL BE WITH YOU WHEREVER YOU GO.

JOSHUA 1:8-9

Within the covers of this single book are all the answers to all the problems that face us today, if we would only look there.

RONALD REAGAN

And the words of the LORD are flawless, like silver refined in a furnace of clay, purified seven times.

PSALM 12:6

The law of the LORD is perfect, reviving the soul.

PSALM 19:7

For the word of the LORD is right and true; he is faithful in all he does.

PSALM 33:4

"Is not my word like fire," declares the LORD," "and like a hammer that breaks a rock in pieces?"

JEREMIAH 23:29

Then you will know the truth, and the truth will set you free.

JOHN 8:32

Jesus answered, "It is written: 'Man does not live on bread alone, but on every word that comes from the mouth of God.'"

MATTHEW 4:4

Therefore everyone who hears these words of mine and puts them into practice is like a wise man who built his house on the rock.

MATTHEW 7:24

Sanctify them by the truth; your word is truth.

JOHN 17:17

But these are written that you may believe that Jesus is the Christ, the Son of God, *and that by believing you may have life in his name.*

JOHN 20:31

P— R— O— M— I— S— E— S—

Seven Secrets
of Memorizing Scripture Verses

1. It's easier than you think!
2. God will bless your efforts!
3. Organization is half the journey!
4. Consistency produces results!
5. It can be fun and exciting!
6. Benefits last for eternity!
7. It's always worthwhile!

To read God's Word a few minutes a day, or even a few minutes a week, is not going to cut it. It's not fair to God or to you. You've got to set yourself up in the best way possible to become more familiar with His truths.

If God's Word is truly a priority, then it should be a priority in our lives. It's easier than you may think.

The challenge is before you. No matter how much of God's Word you know or can find or recollect right now, you can learn more about Jesus in God's Word by choosing methods that work best for you.

It may be intimidating for some to have a goal of memorizing a lot of verses, but with initiative and effort, mixed with the Holy Spirit's guidance and perserverance, God's Word promises you that His Word will become even more alive.

Bible verses are not to be taken lightly and they are literally God's loving truth delivered to us to execute change of obedience and redemption in our lives. Thus, from this day forward, God's Word shall become a bigger commitment and priority in our lives.

Let's not believe the devil's lie that Bible study is not a priority, or that familiarizing yourself with God's Word is hard to do. At least test yourself and challenge yourself to look into the new avenues and new ways that God's Word becomes more relevant and more meaningful to you.

You need to find one or two methods that really click for you, that initially and prayerfully expand your vision to familiarizing yourself with scripture.

— DAVE DAVIDSON

This book will keep you from sin, OR sin will keep you from this book.
D. L. MOODY

"Now I commit you to God and to the word
of his grace, which can build you up and give you
an inheritance among all those who are sanctified."
ACTS 20:32

For everything that was written in the past
was written to teach us,
so that through endurance and the
encouragement of the Scriptures
we might have hope.
ROMANS 15:4

Let the word of Christ dwell in you richly
as you teach and admonish one another
with all wisdom, and as you sing psalms,
hymns and spiritual songs with gratitude
in your hearts to God. And whatever you do,
whether in word or deed, do it all in the
name of the Lord Jesus, giving thanks
to God the Father through him.
COLOSSIANS 3:16-17

We must pay more careful attention, therefore,
to what we have heard, so that we do not drift away.
HEBREWS 2:1

Like newborn babies, crave pure spiritual milk,
so that by it you may grow up in your salvation,
now that you have tasted that the Lord is good.
1 PETER 2:2-3

The Holy Scriptures
are our letters from home.
ST. AUGUSTINE

No man can use his Bible
with power unless
he has the character
of Jesus in his heart.
ALAN REDPATH

For the word of God is living and active,
sharper than any two edged sword . . .
it judges the thoughts and attitudes
of the heart.
HEBREWS 4:12

Accept instruction from his mouth
and lay up his words in your heart.
JOB 22:22

an idea whose time has .com
For more stuff on familiarizing yourself with God's Word

VerseRehearse.com
Your Online Referable Resource For Those
SEEKING GOD'S WORD

Scripture
The Secret Of Falling In Love With Jesus Forever . . .
Honor Him Fearfully & Keep His Promises Faithfully

In Psalm 119 David wrote, "I have hidden Your word in my heart that I might not sin against Thee." David knew this was the key to enable him to follow God with deep devotion.

Fran Paris said, "God's Word will always direct our decisions and actions so that, no matter what confronts us, we won't have to panic or feel lost."

As you meditate on God's Word you will start to develop a passion for the Lord that is guaranteed to be a heart-changer.

These commandments that I give you today are to be upon your hearts. Impress them on your children. Talk about them when you sit at home and when you walk along the road, when you lie down and when you get up.
DEUTERONOMY 6:6-8

E-MAIL (ETERNAL-MAIL) FROM JESUS

To: teens@8promises.com

The Bible is a reflection of my heart and my love for you. Through the Holy Spirit, godly men were inspired to write words that reveal my Father's plan for your life.

When you read from the bible you are reading my love letters to you. My love for you is perfect and complete. I will always be with you — you have My Word on it.

The Living Word, Jesus

Think WOW Promise Plan™

Think WOW: Imagine sitting down with God and hearing His perspective on world history, future events, and your life. Well, you don't have to imagine — just sit down and read your Bible.

Make a VOW: Become a student of scripture. Make and keep the promise to grow in God's Word. Put some motion in your devotion by meditating on God's commandments throughout the day.

Plan HOW: Plan for a daily Bible study. Select some power memory verses and carry 3 x 5 cards with these verses everywhere you go. Decide on a plan to read the entire Bible in one year.

Do It NOW: Open your Bible right now. Read, study, and meditate. Ask God in prayer to guide you to scripture passages that will minister to you today. Make His Word a part of your life.

Push the PLOW: Stay rooted in God's Word. Plant the seeds of scripture in your heart. Reinforce daily habits of Bible study and devotion. Be consistent and follow through with your faith.

BIBLIOGRAPHY

Anderson, Neil and Dave Park. *The Bondage Breaker: Youth Edition*. Eugene, OR: Harvest House Publishers, Inc., 1994.

Crabb, Larry. *Finding God*. New York: Walker and Company, 1994.

Davidson, Dan & Dave (Cyrano De Words-u-lac). *If I Could Live My Life Again*. Tulsa, OK: Honor Books, 1995.

Dobson, James. *Life on the Edge*. Dallas, TX: Word Publishing, 1995.

Duewel, Wesley L. *Measure Your Life*. Grand Rapids, MI: Zondervan Publishing House, 1992.

Green, Keith. *Why YOU Should Go To the Mission Field*. Last Days Ministries Tract.

Harris, Joshua. *I Kissed Dating Goodbye*. Sisters, OR: Multnomah Publishers, Inc., 1998.

Hartman, Bob. *More Power To Ya*. Cincinnati, OH: Standard Publishing, 1997.

Malyon, Matt. "Positively Ambiguous". Bringing It Back Home Songs, 1994.

Paris, Fran. *Who Needs Quiet Time? You Do*! Last Days Ministries tract.

Ravenhill, Leonard. *Prayer*. Last Days Ministries tract.

Ravenhill, Leonard. *The Judgment Seat of Christ*. Last Days Ministries tract.

Phillips, Keith. *The Making Of A Disciple*. Fleming H. Revell Company, 1981

Pratney, Winkie. *The Holy Bible Wholly True*. Last Days Ministries tract.

Sievright, Melody Green. *Unsung Heroes*. Last Days Ministries tract.

St. James, Rebecca. *40 Days With God*. Cincinnati, OH: Standard Publishing,1996.

St. James, Rebecca. *You're the Voice: 40 More Days With God*. Cincinnati, OH: Standard Publishing, 1997.

Stowell, Joseph M. *Eternity*. Chicago, IL: Moody Press, 1995.

DAN DAVIDSON
DanDavidson.com
DAVE DAVIDSON
DaveDavidson.com

Along with writing over a dozen books
together, brothers Dan & Dave Davidson
share the mission statement of

T.I.M.E.
Teach, Inspire, Motivate and Encourage.
Using hope and humor they help others reflect on life.

The Davidsons have founded dozens of innovative web
sites. For a current list of their books and materials,
visit their site ThinkWOW.com. They also operate the
evangelistic website 2Heaven.com and have written the
gospel tract, "From Here To Heaven."

Dave attended Moody Bible Institute and Dan earned a
degree in Youth Ministries and Christian Education from
Valparaiso University.

Dan, a Virginia chiropractor, is married to Kimberly and
they have three children, Jacob, Noah and Kirsti. Dave
is a professional photographer and works with autistic
and mentally handicapped adults in Iowa. He and his
wife, Joan, have two sons, Nathan and Joshua.

Dan and Dave are available for speaking engagements
for such topics as the 8 P.R.O.M.I.S.E.S., God's Great
Ambition, and Tracking Your Life Story Inventory. If
you would like more information on having Dan and
Dave speak at your church, convention, or youth group,
visit SpeakYeFirst.com or call (540) 989-0592.

an idea whose time has.com
For more stuff on the 8 P.R.O.M.I.S.E.S. check out
8Promises.com
Prayer Relationships Obedience Ministry Image Sex Eternity Scripture

PROUDLY DISPLAY YOUR P.R.O.M.I.S.E.S.

INSPIRATIONAL POCKET CARD

$0.79 RETAIL

UPC 713438-10912-1

3-1/2 x 2-1/4 LAMINATED

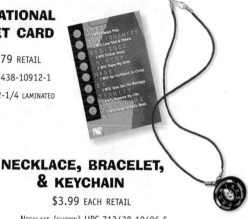

NECKLACE, BRACELET, & KEYCHAIN

$3.99 EACH RETAIL

NECKLACE (SHOWN) UPC 713438-10406-5

BRACELET UPC 713438-10407-2

KEYCHAIN UPC 713438-10408-9

1" DIAMETER, CLAY W/CLOTH CORD

NOTEPAD/PEN SET

THIS THREE-HOLE DRILLED, FOUR-COLOR NOTEPAD IS THE
PERFECT PLACE TO JOG DOWN NOTES FROM THE BOOK,
PRAYER REQUESTS, PHONE NUMBERS, AND SCRIPTURE!

$5.99 RETAIL

UPC 713438-10955-8

8-1/2 x 11, 3-HOLE DRILLED

P.R.O.M.I.S.E.S. KIT

ISBN: 0-89221-476-7

Each kit includes:

1- Notebook Pad

1- Book

1- Bracelet, keychain,
   or necklace

1-Pocket Card

1-Writing Pen

$10.99

(Retail Value $14.76)

•• Notes ••